# Razzle Dazzle Writing

# Razzle Dazzle Writing:

## Achieving Excellence Through 50 Writing Target Skills

## Melissa Forney

Razzle Dazzle Writing
Achieving Excellence Through 50 Target Skills

Cover design: *Maria Messenger*
Layout design: *Billie J. Hermansen*

Library of Congress Cataloging-in-Publication Data
Forney, Melissa, 1952-
    Razzle dazzle writing : achieving success through 50 target skills / Melissa Forney.
        p. cm.
    Inccludes bibliographical references.
    ISBN 0-929895-48-7
    1. English language--Composition and exercises--Study and teaching (Elementary)  2. Language arts (Elementary) I.  Title

LB1576.F6335 2001
372.6'044--dc21                                                    .

2001030162

ISBN-13: 978-0-929895-48-2

Other Professional Resources by Melissa Forney
  *Dynamite Writing Ideas*
  *The Writing Menu*
  *Primary Pizzazz Writing*

Fiction by Melissa Forney
  *A Medal for Murphy*
  *Oonawasse Summer*
  *To Shape a Life*

Maupin House Publishing, Inc.
2416 NW 71st Place
Gainesville, FL 32653
Phone: 800-524-0634
Fax: 352-373-5546
E-mail: info@maupinhouse.com

www.maupinhouse.com

20 19 18 17 16 15 14 13 12

# CONTENTS

# CONTENTS

# CONTENTS

## Personal Narratives

## Expository Writing

## Revising

# CONTENTS

## Revising, cont'd.

## Editing

## Young Author's List of Common Spelling Words

## Writing Assessment

## Resources

# Dedication

For Mary Gunter, a role model for us all.

And for Jane Buss, in whose footsteps I follow.

# Acknowledgments

I would like to thank those who have been a special encouragement to me over the long course of writing this book: my mother, Jacquelyn Forrest, my mother-in-law, Charlotte Forney, Mary Lawson, and Margaret Webb.

For their part in feedback, support, and field testing, I would like to thank Sharon Tanner, J.P. Royer, Gloria Flanagan, Carol Ann Darnell, Jo McGinnis, Dave Scott, Ines Schmook, Myra Seinberg, Lynn Tomlinson, Leigh Austin, Oscar Aguirre, and Missy Beckford.

Also, a special word of appreciation to Jennifer Grzeskowiak, who insisted I write a book of writing mini-lessons for busy teachers. Your vision carried the day.

Most of all, I wish to express my deepest gratitude to my husband and partner, Rick Forney, for his loving help, tireless editing, and constant support.

# Introduction

You've taught your heart out.

You've explained beginning, middle, and ending. You have gone over grabbers and coached conclusions. You've edited until the cows come home. You have read more essays than you can shake a stick at. You've perused piles of poetry, reams of reports, stacks of stories, and a plethora of plays. You have graded until you're jaded and assessed until you're stressed.

Your students have concentrated, deliberated, cooperated, and generated. They've revised, summarized, organized, alphabetized, and capitalized.

Yet still something is lacking. Their writing is so...average. Mundane. Ordinary. What is the missing element? Writing target skills. The "party clothes" of good writing. Razzle Dazzle Writing.

Good writing is more than just what we say. It is also *how we say it.*

Teaching
Razzle Dazzle
Writing

# Teaching Razzle Dazzle Mini-Lessons

Unfortunately, many children dread writing. They don't want to do it, they don't want to learn about it, and most of all, they don't want to revise it. And yet, throughout their lives, they will need to draw upon their ability to communicate through writing. Writing is a foundational skill that enhances all education.

Innovative writing teachers change their student's dread of writing into anticipation and success. Their classrooms are filled with laughter, collaboration, and victorious accomplishment. Successful writing abounds.

These *Razzle Dazzle Writing* mini-lessons have been designed to help students enjoy learning more about the craft of writing. Their purpose is to equip teachers with cutting-edge strategies that improve writing scores and create mature, motivated writers. To help you organize your teaching and lesson plans, mini-lessons have been created for 50 crucial writing target skills young authors will be called on to use (**writing target skills** is a term developed by Marcia Freeman in *Building a Writing Community*, 1995). The mini-lessons can be used in conjunction with any balanced literacy program.

## The Purpose of the Mini-Lessons

The lessons have been designed to help students in grades three through eight improve 50 key writing target skills. Each individual target skill is amplified by definitions and examples. **The mini-lessons are meant to be duplicated for your students and kept in their writing notebooks for future reference.**

Some mini-lessons, with definitions, explanations and examples, are designed to be read aloud as a class. Others are exercises, which students can use to put into practice what they have learned. Some of the mini-lesson pages are Young Author's Lists, intended as references. These lists are specific categories of words that young authors can access while they are writing. Still other mini-lessons involve poetry, to aid retention of knowledge; drama, to increase understanding; and graphic organizers, to involve kinesthetic experiences. Care has been given to address a variety of learning styles, interests, and preferences. The lessons have been field tested with teachers and students over several years, and used to help a number of schools improve assessment scores.

Teaching Razzle Dazzle...continued

# Building Skill Upon Skill

The mini-lessons are arranged by target skills, genres, revising, editing, resources, and assessment. **It is not intended that all of these skills should be taught in one year.** *Razzle Dazzle Writing* is a source of mini-lessons that can be used over the course of several years, according to the abilities and needs of your students. The ideal would be to begin teaching a few of these target skills to fledgling writers and continue, year after year, building skill upon skill, as they grow and mature.

You may mix and match mini-lessons according to your teaching needs, lesson plans, and grade level. However, you will notice that there are several mini-lessons for most target skills, each designed to build on the previous one. It is a good idea to teach each individual writing target skill's mini-lessons in sequence.

Take strong verbs, for example. There is a mini-lesson to *explain* strong verbs. There is a three-minute play *about* strong verbs. There is a mini-lesson *poem* about strong verbs, and there is a mini-lesson Young Author's *List* of strong verbs. **These four mini-lessons should be taught in sequence to foster mastery.**

Each day you teach writing, or during your writing workshops, set aside eight to ten minutes at the beginning of the session to teach, review, or practice one specific writing target skill. This can be done with the entire class or in small groups. **Some target skills may require careful explanation and several days or weeks for students to master. Others can be mastered quickly and implemented immediately.**

Encourage students to use newly-mastered target skills in their writing. Ask them to keep a collection of writing pieces in their writing notebooks. These can be stories, personal narratives, informative writing---a variety of pieces they've worked on before. This way, when they learn a new target skill, they can practice applying it to their writing by inserting that particular skill in a writing piece they already have.

# Preparing for Writing Assessment Tests

Many teachers are now faced with the daunting task of preparing students for state-mandated writing assessment tests. Unfortunately, some teachers and schools are judged or rated by the scores their students earn. **As a result, more emphasis is being put on assessment scores than on learning writing as personal expression and creativity.** This is too bad. When students are assessed, there is usually a great deal of pressure for them to achieve the highest scores possible.

**The target skills taught in this book add razzle dazzle, beauty, depth, and maturity to assessed writing as well as non-assessed writing.**

# Teaching Tips
## Writing Target Skill Plays

*Razzle Dazzle Writing* includes six short, original plays, each of which teaches a different writing target skill. These plays can be performed with script in hand while the rest of the class follows along. They can be presented for other classes, on video, or for parents.

 ## Cast of Characters

### Strong Verb vs. Weak Verb
p. 21

Announcer
Weak Verb
Strong Verb
Groupie Girl

### Simile City
p.27

Miles Magnum
Jane Doe

### META-4 News
p.35

Chuck Roast
Terri Cloth
Ace Weatherman

### Detail Court
p. 96

Bailiff
Judge Trudy
District Attorney
Writing Teacher
Defense Attorney
Student
Sergeant Strongwill

### Who Wants to be a Gazillionaire
p. 128

Regis Filibuster
Monica Stillman
Norma McCraw

### Mission: Possible
p.134

Ian
Emile
Samantha
Dirk
Tape

## Poetry

It has been said that we remember rhyme and verse longer than any other form of learning device. The learning poems in *Razzle Dazzle Writing* are designed for children to memorize in order to facilitate long-range retention of knowledge.

## Lists

There are a number of original lists throughout the book. They are entitled "Young Author's List of..." and have been designed for students to keep as ready references in their writer's notebooks.

Teaching Tips...continued

# Thumbnail References

Thumbnail references have been added to the corners of each page. These guides can help you locate genres, target skills, poems, crafts, lists, etc., quickly. For a more exhaustive reference, refer to the Contents, p. v, or the Index, p. 170.

# The Story Glove

Some teachers consider expository writing and personal narratives easier genres to teach than fictional narratives because they lend themselves to graphic organizers and structure. The Story Glove, p. 62, has been designed as a graphic organizer for fictional narratives to go along with fictional prompts. It can be used to help students cover the basic elements of telling good stories.

The Story Glove comes with an explanation sheet and a craft sheet so students can first learn about the Story Glove and then make one to keep on their desks as a reference. Although the subsequent mini-lessons on fictional narratives were designed to explain and facilitate the use of the Story Glove, they can also be used independently.

# Spelling and Conventions

Spelling is always an issue. It would be a perfect world if children could spell most common words correctly. However, when young writers are composing and creating, it's more important for them to get their thoughts on paper than to stop and look up each word they don't know how to spell. That's where temporary spelling comes into play. Later, during the editing process, they can take the time to correct spelling.

To help children with basic words, a Young Author's List of Common Spelling Words has been included on pp. 146-158. While there are some words that will be found on the Dolch list, and other classic word lists, the list in *Razzle Dazzle Writing* is an original, extended list for young authors. It is meant to be duplicated and used in their writer's notebooks. Students may add additional words to the list on p. 158, or by listing them alphabetically throughout the list.

# Creativity and Creative Writing

All writing we teach to children should be considered *creative writing*. There is not one genre designated for beauty and writing target skills and another for lifeless, unimaginative writing. Encourage students to use target skills in *every* genre of writing.

# Fictional Narrative vs. Personal Narrative

This book makes the distinction between fictional narratives and personal narratives. Fictional narratives are stories based on imaginative experiences and can be written in the first or third person. These stories can be totally fiction or fictionalized accounts of historical or significant events.

Personal narratives are accounts of events or experiences that have happened to the author and are always written in the first person. Personal narratives are sometimes called narrative essays. Some educators classify them as expository writing because, like expository writing, they explain information. Other educators classify personal narratives as narrative writing because, like stories, they have a chronological order and show the passing of time. For the purpose of clarity, this book teaches personal narratives as a hybrid of both fictional and expository writing and teaches it as a separate genre.

# Prompted Writing vs. Free Writing

Throughout *Razzle Dazzle Writing* you will notice many references to writing prompts and prompted writing. While it is necessary to teach students how to respond to writing prompts for assignments and assessment, the author does not wish to give the impression that students should always be given writing prompts, subjects, or specific direction of topics. A key component in learning to write and learning to love writing is the experience of choosing your own topics, genres, styles, and interests. It is recommended that students have many opportunities for free writing and self-expression that also incorporate target skills.
☆☆☆ **Above all, do not use these mini-lessons as "busy work," "seatwork," or a substitute for good teaching and classroom discussions.**

# Graphic Organizers

Five fun projects---all graphic organizers---have been included for your students to use and enjoy.

| Graphic Organizer | Page | Supplies |
|---|---|---|
| The Story Glove | p. 63 | scissors, glue stick, popsicle stick, cardboard |
| The Folded Book | p. 77 | 8.5" x 11" paper, scissors |
| Who, What, When, Where, Why & How Cards | p. 120 | colored card stock, scissors, laminator |
| The Sentence Stretcher | p. 122 | 8.5" x 11" paper, scissors, glue stick, pencil |
| The Sentence Amplifier | p. 137 | colored card stock, scissors, brass brad |

# Teaching Target Skills

Children can learn almost anything if it is broken down into individual steps. By teaching the writing target skills with the Five-Step Skill Method, we help children learn new information, retain knowledge, and apply it to their writing.

## Five-Step Skill Method

 **Explain** Talk to your students. Explain the importance of the skill you are about to teach. Show examples of the finished product as you explain.

 **Demonstrate** Let your students watch you complete the skill. As you demonstrate, encourage students to pay close attention. Repeat the demonstration as needed.

 **Model** Ask your students to do the skill along with you. You may have them do it corporately as a class, in small groups, with partners, or individually.

 **Practice** Allow time for students to practice the skill as many times as needed for mastery. Encourage students to practice the skill at home, too.

 **Teach** Ask students to teach the new skill to someone else, preferably an adult. This step helps children process the information and commit the knowledge to memory.

# Keeping Writing Records

At the heart of this book are the 50 writing target skills and the target skills checklist (p. 9). As your young writers mature into authors, keep records of their progress and chart their personal growth. Teachers, as well as students, should have individualized copies of the target skills checklist. To the side of the checklist columns are four boxes. They correspond to the words Taught, Tested, Applied and Applied.

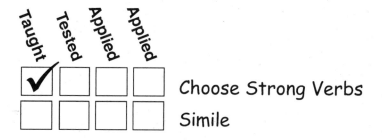

## Taught

Kids like to keep records of skills they have mastered. As you teach each individual target skill with the Five-Step Skill Method, ask your students to check off the box which corresponds to that skill. After you have explained, demonstrated, modeled, and encouraged students to practice, ask them to teach the skill to someone else, preferably an adult, such as a parent, family member, or friend.

## Tested

Testing a target skill takes only a few minutes and can be done on thin strips of paper. Test one isolated skill at a time, for example, similes. Ask students to write a sentence that contains a simile on any subject. They would then check off the corresponding box on their checklists if they have an appropriate answer. Establish, in advance, what you are looking for in an answer: complete sentence, punctuation, and a simile. Some students will require remediation and retesting.

## Applied

The real proof of mastery is when your students correctly apply the target skills they have learned to their own writing, adding depth, maturity, creativity, and beauty. As you discover these skills being used, through assessment and observation of student writing, check off the applied box. Two boxes have been provided for multiple applications.

# Writing Target Skills Checklist

Name _____

Columns for each skill: Applied | Applied | Tested | Taught (all blank checkboxes)

26. Staying in First or Third Person
27. List of Details
28. Supporting with Reasons and Details
29. Basic Expository Paragraph
30. Organizing Multiple Paragraphs
31. Five-Paragraph Essay
32. Expository Grabbers
33. Expository Topic Sentences
34. Introductions
35. Conclusions
36. Restating Information
37. Dialogue in Expository Writing
38. Revising
39. Who, What, When, Where, Why, & How
40. Staying Focused
41. Sizzling Vocabulary
42. Writing Complete Sentences
43. Sentence Variety
44. Sentence Combining
45. Amplified Writing
46. Avoiding Tacky Expressions
47. Using Basic Punctuation
48. Writing Catchy Titles
49. Spelling Common Words Correctly
50. Using a Young Author's Assessment Checklist

Columns for each skill: Applied | Applied | Tested | Taught (all blank checkboxes)

1. Skipping Lines
2. Painting a Word Picture
3. "Show, Don't Tell"
4. Strong Verbs
5. Juicy Color Words
6. Similes
7. Onomatopoeia
8. Specific Emotion and Sensory Words
9. Metaphors
10. Transitional Words and Phrases
11. Writing and Punctuating Dialogue
12. Dialogue with Special Tags
13. Tagless Dialogue
14. Fictional Narrative Prompts
15. Personal Narrative Prompts
16. Expository Prompts
17. Addressing a Prompt
18. Temporary Spelling
19. Jotting
20. Story Glove
21. Narrative Grabber
22. Problem or Challenge
23. Action of the Story
24. Creating Satisfying Solutions
25. Takeaway Endings

# Skipping Lines

Students sometimes crowd their writing, which leads to frustration. Cramming too much on the page is bad news. There is no room to add additions or changes during revision. When writers skip lines during the writing process, they allow room for important revision and editing. Regular notebook paper is not very conducive to skipping lines. Students forget.

The solution is to use **graybar paper**. You'll find a sample on the next page of this book. You may copy that page as a pattern and duplicate it on your copier. Or, make your own graybar pattern on your computer's desktop publishing program. One-half inch bars of gray and white work nicely and allow for several "layers" of revision.

Your students can write on the gray bars and skip the white bars, or the other way around. Either way, they'll find it easier to leave room for **revising** and **editing**. Rough drafts are much easier to write on paper that has ample space between the lines. This allows students to go back, at some future date, and improve and add to their writing.

**Revising:** Revising refers to the big changes an author makes to his rough draft. This means adding more information, adding target skills, or clarifying meaning by choosing more precise words. Revising is done in several stages, or layers, after an author reads his piece aloud to himself and carefully considers content, meaning, and word choice. It's a good idea for students to share their rough drafts in small groups and offer each other feedback and suggestions. If you let some time go by between revisions, your students will be able to see their writing from a fresh viewpoint.

**Editing:** Editing refers to the small changes an author makes before publishing. Editing involves conventions such as correct punctuation and spelling, checking for omitted or duplicated words, grammar, neatness, margins, etc. **Students should not move on to the editing stage until they have revised their piece at least three to five times.** We want young authors to focus on content and creativity, not perfection or neatness. The teaching of good writing is about what a student has to say and how he says it.

A target is printed at the top of each page. Ask your students to choose two or three target skills they have mastered, to include in their rough drafts, and write the initials for them under the target. As they include these skills in their writing, they can draw an arrow coming out of the bull's eye (Marcia Freeman, *Building a Writing Community*, 1995).

The double boxes at the top of the graybar paper pattern are for those times when writing will be scored with a rubric. The first box is for the original score, and the second is for rescoring after students have revised and improved.

Name_____Date_____

Graybar

Razzle Dazzle Writing

# Razzle Dazzle Feedback

Every writer, young and old, enjoys positive feedback about his writing. When you see progress and accomplishment, encourage your students by giving enthusiastic praise.

What a refreshing point of view! Why didn't I think of that?

You make it seem so easy. Would you be willing to help the others?

How did you come up with such terrific ideas?

You've grown so much as a writer. Amazing.

Now you're cookin'! Look at those Strong Verbs.

You write like *magic*. What's your secret?

This has to be the best thing I've read in a long time. Incredible.

I couldn't put your story down until I'd read all the way to the end.

Your writing is a good example of imagination and creativity!

I couldn't be any more proud of you. Thanks for doing your very best.

I don't think a professional writer could have written a better story.

I must share this with the rest of the class. This is a *jewel!*

This is what I mean by *maturity*.

Get ready for fame and fortune!

I know adults who don't write this well.

Your readers are going to eat this up.

You are a genius when it comes to original ideas.

This is just what I've been looking for. A perfect example.

Your writing shows tremendous promise. I have goosebumps.

I hope you're planning to go to college! You have a great future ahead of you.

Your story went straight to my heart. It touched me deeply.

You have such a way with words.

You painted a visual picture. I can see just what you're talking about.

You made me feel like I was right there in your story. I'm *still* scared!

Stupendous. There is no other word to describe this except stupendous.

Think of how far you've come as a writer. Your piece has incredible impact.

I will never forget this piece for as long as I live.

Your writing abilities spell S-U-C-C-E-S-S.

That's it! You've hit the bull's eye this time.

Finally! A kid who knows how to be original.

I would give anything to write like you.

Wait till your parents read this!

Your story would make a great movie. It held me spellbound.

Your supporting details would hold up in court better than most lawyers'.

This piece was difficult, but you didn't let that stop you.

You are beyond funny! I can't stop laughing. Call a doctor.

Sensational...that's all I can say. SENSATIONAL!

It isn't every day a kid leaves her teacher speechless. Wow!

Your enthusiasm makes it easy to be your teacher. You love to write!

There should be a law against writing that's this fantastic.

You are living proof that kids have the best ideas in town.

Remember me when you're world-famous. You're going to the top!

Hard work really pays off, doesn't it? What an accomplishment.

# NOTES

# Writing
# Target Skills

# Painting a Word Picture

Name_____ Date_____

Some writers have the ability to make you see, hear, smell, and imagine things you've never experienced before. How do they do this? Magic? Well, sort of.

**When writers choose words that create mental pictures for the reader, it is called *painting a word picture.*** Have you ever read a book before you saw the movie of the same story? Sometimes the characters and scenes you pictured in your mind were even better than the movie version. This is usually because the writer painted word pictures of what he wanted you to visualize, and your imagination took over from there.

In the following phrases you'll find some similes, metaphors, and picturesque language that help create vivid mental pictures:

...madder than a wet hen
...as mean as a junkyard dog
...so in love she was floating 12 inches off the ground
...as nervous as a cat in a room full of rocking chairs
...as free as a butterfly just out of its cocoon
...faster than a runaway train engine
...he sputtered his words one syllable at a time
...she twisted her hands and bit her lip in frustration
...he nearly popped the buttons off his shirt
...as jumpy as a room full of kindergartners
...the strange, dusky lilac of twilight
...stronger than eight oxen pulling together
...The full moon, a big ball of butter, shone down on the lake.
...as calm as a lake on a windless morning
...the surface of the water glittered like a thousand mirrors
...She's the cream in my coffee.
...His heart nearly jumped out of his chest and his
    blood turned to ice water.
...The dragon's breath smelled like your worst nightmare.
...a stained-glass slice of fruitcake

# Word Picture Poems
by Melissa Forney

Name_____Date_____

Can you use word pictures in all kinds of writing? You bet! Here are some examples of word picture poems that cause the readers' imaginations to go wild.

### M-m-m Delicious
French-fried spiders, pickled frogs,
Candied lizards, sautéed hogs,
Anaconda, served on rice,
Flavored with a pinch of spice.
Buttered skunk with llama sauce,
Salamander served on moss,
Alligator, freshly grilled,
Sea-slug salad nicely chilled,
Marinated monkey meat.
What a feast! Come on, let's eat!

### Dirty Dishes
Piled up high in stacks so grimy,
Crusty, greasy, slick and slimy,
Saucers, glasses, pots and pans,
Scrubbing, scraping, dish pan hands;
Sudsy water, wet and steamy,
Dried up eggs and sauces, creamy,
If I could have a single wish,
I'd never wash another dish!

### Greasy Old Stuff
Under the car hood there's greasy old stuff,
Hoses and fan-belts all rubbery and rough.
Gadgets are grinding and pistons are pumping,
And some little gizmo is spinning and thumping.
The engine is coughing a frightful explosion;
The battery's covered with gray-green corrosion.
Gas fumes are rising and motors are whirring
And what-cha-ma-call-its are chugging and purring.

### Get Me Out of Here!
Shots and needles, tables and lights,
Sirens, doctors, nurses in white.
Tongue depressors, casts and stitches,
Rashes, fractures, pains and itches.
Paramedics, ambulances,
Frantic families, worried glances.
Children grouchy, babies sleepy,
Get me out of here---it's creepy!

### Mud
It squishes up between your toes
And squirts around your feet;
Some people think that mud is gross
But me? I think it's neat.

# "Show, Don't Tell"

Name_____Date_____

**"Show, Don't Tell" means to describe something for your readers instead of telling them something too obvious.** For instance, here is a sentence that just tells:

## The boy was very frightened.

There's no wondering about it: you have been told the boy was frightened. But notice the difference when the writer **shows** the reader what frightened *looks like:*

## The boy screeched in terror and threw his hands up to protect himself. Even though his legs felt like they had turned to jelly, he jumped to his feet and tried to get out of the monster's reach.

You don't have to tell your readers the boy was frightened. When they read your description of his reactions, they get the picture on their own. This type of descriptive writing makes reading much more fun. Readers like to picture the scene in their own minds. As a writer, you can help them do this by painting a word picture of what the scene looks like. Or, you can describe how a character's body reacts to a specific emotion or situation.

Here's another example. A kid who doesn't know how to "Show, Don't Tell" might write about a crying baby like this:

## The baby was crying really hard.

That's obvious. But what does a crying baby look like? What was the baby doing to let you know she was upset? Notice the difference when the writer describes the scene:

## The baby let out a howl that could wake the dead. Tears poured from her eyes and her face turned beet red. She pounded her little fists on the floor and threw her toys across the room. I knew we were in for a long, long afternoon.

This time, the writer paints a word picture that describes the crying baby much better than the obvious statement above. In narrative or expository writing, don't just *tell* your readers something they don't have to think about. *Show them.* Describe what is going on, someone's physical reaction to an emotional situation, or a sequence of events.

# Practicing "Show, Don't Tell"

Name_____Date_____

Don't be too obvious when you write. That's kind of like explaining a joke after you tell it.  People like to "get it" on their own.

Be creative. Paint word pictures. Decribe the action that is going on or a character's emotional reaction. What does his body do? How does he move? How does he respond?

Look at the following pictures. Describe the scene as if your reader cannot see what's going on. "Show, Don't Tell."

Too obvious:     The kids were disrespectful to the teacher.

"Show, Don't Tell"     _____

_____

_____

_____

_____

_____

_____

Too obvious:     The iguana got away.

"Show, Don't Tell"     _____

_____

_____

_____

_____

_____

_____

# Strong Verbs

Name_____Date_____

Verbs are action words. But did you know there are weak verbs and strong verbs? Young authors need to know the difference between the two.

## WEAK VERB

## STRONG VERB

**Weak verbs are words that have been over-used or don't add any new information to the sentence.** They are okay. They just lack imagination.

weak
The bunny went across the field.

**Strong verbs add more information to the sentence. Strong verbs paint a word picture in the reader's mind and create mature, well-written sentences.**

strong
The bunny scampered across the field.

What a difference! You could have chosen any other strong verb such as:

| | | | |
|---|---|---|---|
| raced | crawled | danced | skipped |
| flew | bolted | zig-zagged | hopped |

Each of these strong verbs would change the sentence and add a completely new meaning. Here's another example of a sentence with a weak verb:

weak
My sister hurt me because I wouldn't let her sit by the window.

The verb hurt is a little weak. You know something painful happened, but you don't know what it was. When you can, it's better to use a verb that *shows* the reader exactly what happened.

strong
My sister pinched my arm when I wouldn't let her sit by the window.

# Strong Verb vs. Weak Verb

A Three-Minute Play by Melissa Forney

**Announcer:** Ladies and Gentlemen! In this corner, weighing in at 99 pounds dripping wet, looking pretty average and puny, we have---Weak Verb!

**Audience:** (mild applause)

**Weak Verb:** Thank you (cough). I'll try to be my adequate, ordinary self. (wheeze)

**Announcer:** "---And in this corner, weighing in at a hefty 250 pounds, that tower of perpetual strength, STROOOOONG VERRRRRRRRRB!!!

**Audience:** (wild applause, whistles, etc.)

**Strong Verb:** I'm the greatest! I'm the champion! I'm what weak verbs *want to be* when they grow up! I bring new meaning to every sentence! I eat weak verbs for breakfast! Fly like a butterfly, sting like a bee! There's not a weak verb that can top me!

**Audience:** (wild applause, cheers, etc.)

**Groupie Girl:** Oooo look! Check out those muscles! (giggles)

**Announcer:** Let's get ready to rumble!! Play fair, no hitting below the belt, and may the best verb win. Round one: Give me a sentence that has "Mom" and "dishes" in it. (bell DING)

**Weak Verb:** I've got it! I've got it! Uh...er...umm...Mom **did** the dishes.

**Announcer:** Yes, that *is* a verb....However---

**Strong Verb:** Let ME try......(pause).....Mom **scrubbed** the dishes.

**Announcer:** And the winner is---Strong Verb! *Scrubbed* is a much stronger verb than *did*.

**Audience:** Strong Verb! Strong Verb! Strong Verb!

**Announcer:** Round two: Give me a sentence that has "Mike" and "party" in it. (bell DING)

**Weak Verb:** I know! I know! Let me see....um...um....Mike **got ready** for the party.

**Strong Verb:** Mike **showered**, **combed** his hair, and **put on** fresh clothes for the party.

**Announcer:** Strong Verb scores a KNOCKOUT with three strong verbs! Ladies and Gentlemen, I give you the champion of the writing world, STROONNG VERRRRRB!!! (bell DING, DING, DING, DING, DING)

**Audience:** Woof! Woof! Woof!

**Weak Verb:** Don't I get any respect? I tried my (cough) very best...I'm a verb--really I am. You've GOT to believe me! I'm just so *weak*...

**Strong Verb:** I am the GREATEST! I am SUPERB!
If you want to score a knockout, use a STRONG VERB!!!! (crowd goes wild!)

**Groupie Girl:** Oh Strongie, could I have your autograph? You're...like...SO strong! (sigh)

# Strong Verb Poem

## The Dog Ate The Bone
by Melissa Forney

The dog **ate** the bone.

Don't you think that's kind of weak?

The verb here is "ate"

But it needs a little tweak.

The dog **ate** the bone,

Let's try another verb.

One that's really fun to write,

One that's quite superb.

The dog could **devour** the bone,

**Nibble**, **gnaw**, or **munch** it.

The dog could **snark-up** the bone,

**Gobble**, **bite** or **crunch** it.

The dog could **consume** the bone,

Oh yes, that dog could do it,

**Inhale** the bone, **impale** the bone,

**Swallow**, **gulp** or **chew** it.

So when you're writing to impress,

Don't use a verb that fizzles.

Think of every word you know,

And give me one that sizzles!

# Young Author's List of Strong Verbs

This list of 180 strong verbs will help you get started on the road to colorful, dazzling writing. Feel free to add other interesting, vivid verbs you find in books, newspapers, and magazines.

| | | | | |
|---|---|---|---|---|
| aimed | devoured | hauled | ransacked | stamped |
| anticipated | diapered | hiccupped | reassured | steamed |
| arranged | disciplined | high-fived | recorded | stitched |
| backpacked | dog paddled | howled | rejoiced | strained |
| backtracked | double-checked | humiliated | relished | stretched |
| ballooned | doused | iced | rescued | strode |
| bamboozled | drained | irritated | ripped | stuffed |
| bandaged | dreaded | jabbed | rocked | tangoed |
| baptized | drooped | jack-knifed | rowed | tap-danced |
| blasted | dusted | juggled | sabotaged | teased |
| blotted | eased | karate chopped | sanded | thawed |
| boiled | ejected | leaped | sassed | throttled |
| bolted | electrocuted | lumbered | sauntered | thundered |
| botched | enfolded | luxuriated | scoured | tickled |
| bounded | enveloped | magnified | scraped | tip-toed |
| bulldozed | erased | manipulated | scratched | toasted |
| bullied | evaporated | meandered | scribbled | trespassed |
| burped | fired | measured | scrubbed | trucked |
| chastised | flattered | melted | shaved | tucked |
| chattered | flipped | monopolized | shivered | twisted |
| chauffeured | flirted | mystified | shrieked | twitched |
| cheapened | focused | oozed | shrugged | viewed |
| cherished | french-braided | outwitted | shuddered | vindicated |
| chuckled | frolicked | papered | side-stepped | volunteered |
| clipped | frosted | parachuted | slam-dunked | waltzed |
| conducted | glowed | pasted | slimed | weighed |
| consoled | goofed | patted | slithered | wiggled |
| constructed | grated | peered | smirked | wiped |
| corked | greased | piggybacked | sneezed | wisecracked |
| crawled | grilled | pitter-pattered | snooped | withered |
| crooned | groaned | plucked | snoozed | wormed |
| cultivated | guaranteed | poached | splattered | worshiped |
| decorated | guffawed | pounded | spliced | wrangled |
| delved | gurgled | praised | splurged | wrenched |
| demolished | hammered | pranced | sprinted | wrinkled |
| despised | harvested | raged | squished | yelped |

# Juicy Color Words

Name_____Date_____

We are fortunate to live in a world splashed with every color imaginable. We are surrounded with a kaleidoscope of shades from every color family, not just red, yellow, blue, green, orange, purple, brown, black, and white. **Juicy color words are names of specific colors.** There are thousands of color words in the English language.

### Red
cherry red
lobster red
crimson red
watermelon red
brick red
candy apple red

### Blue
robin's egg blue
powder blue
sky blue
royal blue
navy blue
denim blue

### Yellow
lemon yellow
goldenrod
mustard yellow
egg yolk yellow
school bus yellow
fluorescent yellow

### Green
olive green
forest green
khaki green
emerald green
lime green
pistachio green

### Purple
lavender
orchid
periwinkle
grape
eggplant
plum

### Orange
pumpkin orange
marigold
sunset orange
fluorescent orange
burnt sienna
caution orange

### Brown
leather brown
chocolate brown
mahogany brown
chestnut brown
coffee brown
camel

### Black
ebony
jet black
charcoal
raven
midnight black
pitch black

### White
snow white
alabaster white
vanilla
eggshell
ivory
pearl

Juicy color words help readers picture an exact description and add pizazz to your writing. **But be careful! When you use juicy color words, they must sound natural. Don't over-use them. One or two words in a piece add just the right amount of description without being too showy.**

# Super-Star Colors

Name_____Date_____

Some **juicy color words** don't fit into any specific color family. They are unusual blends we recognize from the world around us. These colors are so awesome, so dazzling, that they stand alone! We call these **super-star colors**, and they're a great addition to descriptive writing.

## Super-Star Colors

| | | |
|---|---|---|
| rainbow | peppermint | |
| dalmation | chocolate chip | |
| camouflage | pimento cheese | |
| hologram | transparent | |
| confetti | black cherry | |
| multi | Day-Glo | polka dot |
| tutti-fruiti | glow-in-the-dark | stripe |
| Neapolitan | mirror | glitter |
| stained glass | tapestry | tortoise |
| mother-of-pearl | plaid | calico |
| iridescent | opal | blacklight |

Can you think of any other super-star colors? Add them here:

_____          _____

_____          _____

Other super-star word description categories you might want to consider are:

| **Metallic** | **Skin Tones** | **Jewel Tones** |
|---|---|---|
| gold | ivory | diamond |
| silver | peaches 'n cream | emerald |
| platinum | bronze | sapphire |
| bronze | café-au-lait | topaz |
| copper | mahogany | ruby |
| steel | ebony | citrine |

# Similes

Name_____Date_____

My little brother is **as clumsy a bull in a china shop** when he runs through my room!

Mary Ellen acts **like a big baby** when she doesn't get her way.

The sunset looks **like a dazzling watercolor painting.**

Similes, similes, similes. They're everywhere! **When we compare two things, using the words *like* or *as*, it's called a simile.** Picturing something in your mind helps you understand it better. Similes show us the qualities of an object or person by comparing it to something else.

For instance, read the following simile:

K'nesha is as light on her feet as a ballet dancer.

You get a picture in your mind of a dancer's graceful movements.

Whoever K'nesha is, you know she must be graceful. Here's another example:

His grin was as toothy as a great white shark's.

The writer wants you to know his character's smile was toothy, and it's easy to picture when it is compared to a shark's. Try finishing these simile beginnings so your reader gets a vivid picture of what you're trying to describe:

1. Hannah was as mad as _____.

2. Waiting for the doctor, I was as nervous as _____

_____.

3. Mother hyenas protect their young like_____

_____.

4. Manatees, also known as sea cows, are like _____

_____.

# Simile City

A Three-Minute Play by Melissa Forney

**Miles Magnum:** (Private detective voice) It was a city that could break your heart into a million pieces. A city that never sleeps. I was feeling as worn out as an old piece of shoe leather when the phone rang. (Ring, Ring) Hello. You've reached Like-or-As Detective Agency. Miles Magnum, private investigator, speaking.

**Jane Doe:** My name is Jane Doe, Mr. Magnum. I have a problem. A perplexing problem.

**Miles Magnum:** For me, solving problems is like taking candy from a baby.

**Jane Doe:** Well, I'm new in town. Just off the bus from Mundane. I've only been here one day and...(Begins to cry)...everyone's comparing me to things. Why? WHY? (Cries harder)

**Miles Magnum:** (To audience) She was sobbing like a baby with an empty bottle. (To Jane) Comparing you...to things. Can you give me an example, Miss Doe?

**Jane Doe:** (Sniffing) I'll...try...to. I got off the bus yesterday and the bus driver said, "You look as tired as a new mother with triplets."

**Miles Magnum:** I see...

**Jane Doe:** And then, a lady in the hotel lobby said, "Welcome to town, Honey. Why, you're as cute as a button." (Sob) Next, I called an employment agency and after I explained who I was she said, "You sound like a woman who's looking for a job." (Sob) See what I mean? Everyone in town compares me to something!

**Miles Magnum:** I see your dilemma....Hmmm...Let me ask you a question. Do they use the words "like" or "as" when they make these comparisons?

**Jane Doe:** Yes! Oh, Mr. Magnum. How did you know?

**Miles Magnum:** You've got nothing to worry about, Sister. Don't you know what town you're in?

**Jane Doe:** Well, it's a cute little town, but I didn't actually catch the name...

**Miles Magnum:** You're in Simile City, where similes are as common as fleas on a hound dog.

**Jane Doe:** Similes?

**Miles Magnum:** When we compare two things, using the words like or as, it's called a simile. We do it all the time and...it's a very *mature* thing to do, I might add.

**Jane Doe:** So it's not just me? Oh, thank you, Mr. Magnum. I'm as relieved as a patient who's just gotten good news from the doctor. (Cheerfully) Good-bye, and thank you. You've helped me a great deal.

**Miles Magnum:** Any time. Take care of yourself. (To audience) I locked my office and stepped out into the night. It was as cold as a polar bear's nose, but that didn't slow me down. I was from Simile City and I'd just helped a lady in distress. I felt like a million bucks.

# Onomatopoeia Poem

Name_____Date_____

**The "popcorn" of the writing world is *onomatopoeia*, or *sound effect* words.** If used to recreate specific sounds or moods, these fun-to-read words can give your stories, poems, plays, or comic strips just the right zing!

Memorize the poem below to help you remember the meaning of the word and to learn how to spell it.

## ONOMATOPOEIA

by Melissa Forney

Onomatopoeia,
My, what a word!
It means every sound effect
You have ever heard.
Crash, crunch, zing, zip,
Meow, munch, roar, rip,
Sizzle, crackle, splat, kerplunk,
Bang, clank, woof, thunk,
Hiss, whiz, oink, moo,
Sniff, snap, cough, achoo,
Dong, ding, pong, ping,
Bong, bing, zap, zing!
I think that when
you've read this list
You'll get the main idea...
All these crazy sound effects
Are onomatopoeia!
Once you learn to say that word
You kind of want to yell it,
But even though you yell the word
I bet you cannot spell it!
You can learn to spell this word
In just a single day...
O-N-O---M-A-T-O-P-O-E-I-A

POW!

BOOSH!

# Putting Onomatopoeia to Use

Name_____Date_____

When Hollywood makes a movie, a foley artist creates special sound effects so the action will seem real. Onomatopoeia, especially when read aloud, can make your writing come alive just like sound effects in a movie. Read the poem "Roller Coaster" aloud. Listen to the rhythm of the words. Notice how the use of sound effects creates an atmosphere of excitement.

## Roller Coaster
by Melissa Forney

Fasten your seatbelts,
All hands inside,
Everyone aboard for the
Roller coaster ride!
Click-clack, click-clack
Creeping up the hill,
Daredevil laughter,
Ready for the thrill.
S-L-O-W-L-Y, S-L-O-W-L-Y
Cresting the top,
Hands start to tremble,
Hearts almost stop.
Plunge down the steep slope,
Faster than a rocket,

Loose change and sunglasses,
Fly from your pocket.
Swoop round the sharp bend,
Twisting in a loop,
Scream like a Banshee,
Yelling out a whoop!
Sail down the valleys,
Race up the hills,
Nothing else can equal
Roller coaster thrills.
Clickety-clack, clickety-clack,
Round the final bend,
Why does every roller coaster
Have...to...have...an.......end?

Onomatopoeia is just the tool a writer needs to describe sounds made by common objects, animals, or nature. As you read this passage from the novel, *The Blue Tattoo*, by Melissa Forney, listen for sound effect words that help create the scene in the reader's mind.

The water underneath the *River Gem* churned and sputtered and the mighty craft surged forward with a steady chug-woosh-a-chug-chug, chug-woosh-a-chug-chug. The crowd on the dock grew smaller as the boat made its way out into the main current of the Oonawassee. The wind whipped Addie's hair. They were off.

# Creating Onomatopoeia

Name_____Date_____

Here's your chance to create crazy sound effects and put those sounds into letters. Read the categories below and write an onomatopoeia "word" for each one. Everyone's answers will be a little different.

| | | | |
|---|---|---|---|
| 1. bacon cooking | sizzle | 21. a train's steam engine | |
| 2. a crying baby | | 22. a dropped lightbulb | |
| 3. a newborn kitten | | 23. jingle bells | |
| 4. a window breaking | | 24. a hungry lion | |
| 5. popcorn | | 25. someone eating ice | crunch-crack-slurp |
| 6. wild monkeys | oo-oo-oo--OOO | 26. ocean waves | |
| 7. a motor boat | vroom-vroom! | 27. hurricane wind | |
| 8. rain | | 28. a horse | |
| 9. a friendly dog | | 29. marbles | |
| 10. a mean dog | | 30. a basketball | swoosh! |
| 11. an injured dog | hm-hm-hmmm | 31. a zipper | |
| 12. the front door | | 32. tearing cloth | |
| 13. a big bass drum | | 33. a doorbell | |
| 14. a fire engine | | 34. a dentist's drill | |
| 15. bath water | | 35. a rattlesnake | cht-cht-cht-cht |
| 16. an arrow | flup! | 36. a baby chick | |
| 17. a blender | | 37. geese | |
| 18. a bonfire | | 38. a hammer | blam |
| 19. sneezing | | 39. a horse's hooves | |
| 20. an angry alien | | 40. an electric fan | |

# Specific Emotion and Sensory Words

Name_____Date_____

## Specific Emotion Words

People connect with other people through their emotions. Whether you're writing a fictional narrative, personal narrative, an opinion piece or a persuasive piece, it's a good idea to use specific emotion words. **Specific emotion words are words that tell the reader exactly how someone feels.** Some young writers try to do this, but they use words that could mean more than one thing.

General:     Last spring, when our High Achievers Club helped clean up the beach, I felt really **good**.

The word *good* in this sentence could be talking about physical health. Were you just getting over the flu and now you feel better? Or, it could be talking about a specific emotion. Did you feel proud? Helpful? The meaning is unclear, fuzzy.

In this sentence, the writer substitutes **two specific emotion words to give clarity and maturity to the writing:**

Specific:     Last spring, when our High Achievers Club helped clean up the beach, I felt **proud** and **helpful**, like I had contributed something.

## Specific Sensory Words

When an author takes the time to describe something to her readers, she usually wants them to imagine and mentally experience what she's describing. Many young authors use general words to describe the five senses. **General words are words like good, great, terrific, awesome, or bad, terrible, horrible and gross.** These words point the reader towards positive and negative feelings, but they are too general.

Really mature writing uses specific sensory words. **Specific sensory words pinpoint the exact sense, or sensation, you are talking about.**

General:     I didn't eat my sandwich because it tasted **bad**.

Specific:     I didn't eat my sandwich because it tasted **stale**.

# Young Author's List of Specific Emotion Words

Name_____Date_____

One of the reasons we like to read fiction is because we can live many different lives through the characters we read about. Readers like to connect emotionally with characters, so be sure to use specific words that pinpoint feelings.

## Positive Emotions....

accepted
affirmed
appreciated
approved
beautiful
befriended
calm
cheerful
cherished
courteous
ecstatic

empowered
encouraged
exalted
excited
exhilarated
exonerated
exuberant
forgiven
generous
happy
helpful
honored
hopeful
impressed

included
joyful
jubilant
kind
loved
loyal
needed
obedient
overjoyed
patient
praised
prepared
protected
proud

purposeful
recognized
relaxed
respected
revered
reverent
rewarded
safe
secure
sympathetic
trusted
understood
uplifted
useful

## Negative Emotions....

agitated
aloof
ambivalent
angry
ashamed
average
bedraggled
befuddled
belligerent
bereft
betrayed
bewildered
blah
blamed
blase´
blue
bothered
chastised
confused
contrary
crazy
crushed
depressed

discarded
discouraged
discriminated
disgusted
distant
faint
frustrated
guilty
hated
hesitant
hopeless
hostile
humiliated
idiotic
impetuous
implicated
indifferent
insane
insecure
irritated
jilted
laughed at
left-out

lonely
mad
melancholy
mocked
moronic
morose
ornery
out-of-control
out-of-step
overwhelmed
perplexed
picked on
pouty
puny
put down
rebellious
rejected
reviled
revolted
rotten
sad
scared
shattered

sick
slighted
spoiled
spooky
strange
stressed
stubborn
stupid
temperamental
trapped
tumultuous
ugly
unhappy
unprepared
unruly
upset
used
useless
vexed
vulnerable
weak
weary
worn-out

# Young Author's List of Sensory Words

Name_____Date_____

Razzle dazzle your readers by writing with descriptive sensory words.

## Sight

| | | | | |
|---|---|---|---|---|
| black & white | dark | hazy | psychedelic | striped |
| bright | dull | large | round | swaying |
| brilliant | faded | light | shaded | swirling |
| cloudy | flapping | misty | spotted | textured |
| colored | flashing | murky | square | translucent |
| crystal clear | floating | opaque | stained | transparent |
| curved | foggy | pointed | straight | twisted |

## Sound

| | | | | |
|---|---|---|---|---|
| baying | clinking | humming | roaring | splashing |
| beating | crackling | jangling | rustling | sputtering |
| booming | crashing | jingling | scraping | swishing |
| buzzing | dripping | meowing | screeching | ticking |
| chiming | grating | moaning | slurping | wailing |
| chugging | growling | mooing | sneezing | whinnying |
| clanging | honking | popping | snorting | whistling |
| clanking | howling | rev ving | sobbing | whizzing |

## Taste

| | | | | |
|---|---|---|---|---|
| bitter | dry | lemony | rancid | stale |
| bubbly | fishy | moldy | salty | sugary |
| burnt | fresh | nutty | smoky | sweet |
| buttery | garlicy | oily | sour | sweet & sour |
| cheesy | gingery | oniony | spicy | tart |
| chocolatey | juicy | peppery | spoiled | vinegary |

## Smell

| | | | | |
|---|---|---|---|---|
| antiseptic | flowery | mildewy | pungent | salty |
| cheesy | fresh | musky | putrid | sharp |
| dank | fruity | musty | rainy | smoky |
| decayed | gassy | new | rancid | strong |
| dusty | grassy | old | rosy | wet |
| earthy | leathery | perfumey | rotten | woodsy |

## Touch

| | | | | |
|---|---|---|---|---|
| bristly | furry | moist | sandy | starchy |
| brittle | glassy | nubby | silky | steamy |
| cottony | gooey | pleated | slick | sticky |
| crusty | gritty | powdery | slimy | stiff |
| dewy | hairy | puffy | smooth | velvety |
| flexible | metallic | rough | spongy | wiry |

# Metaphors

Name_____Date_____

**Metaphors are tools authors use to make rich comparisons between two things that ordinarily wouldn't be connected.** Metaphors are similar to similes, but they don't use the words *like* or *as*. Notice how these metaphors help the author create a visual picture in the reader's mind.

The tornado became a raging bull, smashing everything in its path.

All animals fear the lion, the king of the jungle, who stalks and kills at will.

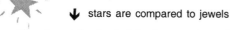
stars are compared to jewels

Sky jewels twinkled overhead in the night sky with elegant splendor.

In order to create a metaphor, first think of something you wish to describe. Picture the description you want to give to the reader. Was the tornado fierce and destructive? Compare it to a raging bull. Do the stars twinkle like jewels? In a metaphor they *become* jewels. Is the lion feared and respected by all others? So are some kings. In a metaphor the lion *becomes* a king. Metaphors can be based on almost any subject you can imagine:

The brilliant rays of the morning sun, the world's alarm clock, stretch and spread across the radiant sky.

The cobra's poison was a time bomb waiting to go off as it spread through Professor Thompson's weakened body.

When I was grounded for a week, my room was a prison of despair.

The delicious lobsters we caught that summer on the Maine coast were gifts from the sea.

Starla pulled the extra quilts around her and nestled in her bed, a warm cave that kept out the winter's chill.

Grandmother was the sunshine of Rebecca's life, the person she could run to in times of trouble.

The calm sea was an endless mirror, reflecting the beauty of the cloud filled sky.

My dad is a polar bear when it comes to swimming in cold water.

# META-4 News

A Three-Minute Play by Melissa Forney

| | |
|---|---|
| Chuck: | Good evening and welcome to Meta-4 News. I'm your anchor, Chuck Roast, alongside my lovely and talented co-anchor, Terri Cloth. |
| Terri: | Why, thank you, Chuck. Let's get right to the heart of the news tonight. There was a six-car pile-up on the interstate earlier this evening. It clogged the main artery of the city for nearly two hours. The tangle of cars has been cleared away now, and traffic is once again flowing. |
| Chuck: | Terri, that interstate will swallow you whole if you're not paying attention to traffic. (pause) Now here's a news story that will knock your socks off. Today, Binky, our beloved hippopotamus, delivered a new bundle of joy at the city zoo. The baby has been named Peaches by zookeeper Hammond Rye. Mr. Rye was heard to comment, "Binky is a whiz when it comes to mothering. Peaches couldn't be in better hands." We welcome our newest citizen. |
| Terri: | Let's shift gears now and go to our ace weatherman, Ace Weatherman. |
| Ace: | Thanks Terri, and let me just say that the weather really stung us again today. One of the causes of that wreck on the interstate was that it was raining cats and dogs. It was truly miserable out there. The wind howled, and lightning danced across the sky. Liquid sunshine will continue to drench us tomorrow morning, so your umbrella will be your best friend and traveling companion. However, by mid-afternoon a smiling Mr. Sun will send those thunder clouds packing and replace them with a knock-out blue sky. Back to you, Chuck. |
| Chuck: | Thanks, Ace. And now, our final story, one that will sadden your taste buds. Big Olaf's Chocolate Emporium burned to the ground early this morning. Fire devoured the entire building before firemen could arrive. Employees managed to escape with only minor injuries. The cause of the fire is still a puzzle, however. Investigators have been hand-cuffed in their attempts to search through the debris due to the nasty weather. Big Olaf's son, Little Lars, who has worked in the fudge room for 37 years, was quoted as saying, "Generations of children will be heartbroken at the loss. This place was a kid's paradise." Terri, what a blow to the entire community. |
| Terri: | Big Olaf's fudge was the love of my life, Chuck. The world will be a little less friendly without that wonderful sweet haven. Let's hope they rebuild. And that's the news for this evening. |
| Chuck: | Join us again tomorrow night for the personification of news, here at station META-4, your johnny-on-the-spot ace reporters. Thank you for joining us. I'm Chuck Roast... |
| Terri: | ...And I'm Terri Cloth. Whether the news is sour or sweet, The team at META-4 can't be beat. We bring you weather, features, and wars And spice up our language with metaphors. |

# Young Author's Metaphor Collection

Name_____

Once you know what to look for, metaphors seem to be everywhere. As you see them in books and magazines and hear them in conversations, write them down. Having a collection of metaphors is a great help when it comes to your own writing.

# Transitional Words and Phrases

Name_____Date_____

When writing moves from one thought to the next, it needs to be smooth. **Transitional words and phrases keep our thoughts from sounding choppy or disjointed.** They can be used in stories, personal narratives, and informational writing of all kinds.

Imagine a long column of dominoes standing on end. When you knock over the first one, each domino falls smoothly into the next one, knocking it down and so on, all the way to the end. If there were gaps in the dominoes, the action would end. Transition words and phrases help writing flow from idea to idea, smoothly and naturally. Some transitions are just one or two words. Others are longer phrases.

The following paragraph is written with no transitions:

My brothers and sister and I have certain jobs we do to help the rest of the members of our family. My main job each week is keeping our van clean. That's a big job. I have to clean out all of the trash. I vacuum under every seat and in the aisles. I clean all of the windows, inside and out, until they shine. I scrub every inch of the outside of the van with hot, soapy water and rinse it with the hose. I dry the van with special towels that don't have any lint. I'm always proud of the way I keep the van clean for my family.

Now let's look at the same paragraph with transitional words and phrases:

My brothers and sister and I have certain jobs we do to help the rest of the members of our family.
trans. phrase
For example, my main job each week is keeping our van clean. By the way, that's a big
trans. phrase                         trans. phrase
job, let me tell you. To begin with, I have to clean out all of the trash. Next, I vacuum
trans. phrase        trans. phrase                              trans. word
under every seat and in the aisles. After that, I clean all of the windows, inside and
trans. phrase
out, until they shine. Then, I scrub every inch of the outside of the van with hot, soapy
trans. word
water and rinse it with the hose. For the final step, I dry the van with special towels
trans. phrase
that don't have any lint. As you can imagine, I'm always proud of the way I keep the
trans. phrase
van clean for my family.

# Young Author's List of Transitions

Be sure you understand the meanings of these transitional words and phrases before you use them. Most of the time they require a comma after them.

After
After a few days
After awhile
After all
After that
After that step
Afterward
All in all
Also
Although
Although it is true
Another example
As a general rule
As a result
As I have said
As soon as
As we have seen
At first
At last
At that time
At the same time
At this point
Because
Because of this
Before
Besides
Beyond
By the same token
By the way
By this time
Consequently
Finally
First
First of all
For an instant
For example
For instance
For now
For one thing
For the time being
From now on
Furthermore
Gradually
However

I'll be the first to admit
If you look at it that way
In a little while
In addition
In any case
In any event
In closing
In conclusion
In fact
In other words
In particular
In the beginning
In the first place
In the same way
Incidentally
Last
Later
Later on
Let me explain.
Let's look at it a different way
Likewise
Looking back
Meanwhile
Moving right along
Naturally
Nevertheless
Next
Now
Obviously
Of course
On the other hand
Once again
Once that is done
Perhaps
Put another way
Second
Simply stated
Since
So then
Sometimes
Soon
Specifically
Suddenly
The first step

The following example
The next step
Then
There is no doubt that
Third
This takes us to
Though
To begin
To begin with
To illustrate my point
To illustrate this
To put it differently
To start off
To sum up my thoughts
Until
Usually
What happened next
When
When all is said and done
When you look at it
    that way
Without warning
You see

## ORDINALS

by Melissa Forney

When you write out directions
    and list the steps to take,
Make sure you get your
    **ordinals** right,
    Don't make a big mistake.
For they are **first** and **second**,
    **third** and **fourth**, you see.
Don't add an "-ly" to the end:
    It is NOT *secondly.*
*Thirdly* makes me shudder,
    *Fourthly* makes me scoff,
So write them **second**, **third**
    and **fourth**,
    And leave the "-ly" off.

# Writing Dialogue

Name_____Date_____

You can find out many things about a person by listening to what he says. You can also learn interesting tidbits of information or understand certain characters better. **Writing down what people say is called *dialogue*. Dialogue can be complete sentences or just a word or two.**

Adding dialogue to your stories makes them much more interesting. Your readers don't just want to know what your main character *does;* they also want to know what he *says.* Writing conversation for your characters makes them seem more believable.

## Without Dialogue

Toni cradled the horse's head in her arms and whispered softly into his ear. She told Rembrandt how much she loved him. She promised she would never sell or leave him. His wide, liquid eyes never left hers.  He nuzzled her hand. Toni was sure he understood.

## With Dialogue

Toni cradled the horse's head in her arms and whispered softly into his ear. "Hey, Boy...hey. I love you. Know that?" His wide, liquid eyes never left hers. "And don't worry, cause I'm never going to sell you. I'm never going to leave you." He nuzzled her hand. "Yeah...You understand, don't you, Boy."

The first paragraph tells us what Toni and Rembrandt *did.* The second paragraph also allows us to *hear* the tender things Toni says to her horse. The dialogue makes us feel as if we are standing right by Toni and Rembrandt, listening to their intimate conversation.

**The key to writing good dialogue is to sound natural. Pay attention to the way people speak. Sometimes they don't speak in complete sentences, and sometimes they speak in incomplete phrases.** Their words might reflect their age, their emotions, or where they're from. When you write dialogue for your characters, keep these things in mind. Try to write dialogue that sounds realistic.

A word of caution: sometimes young writers write far too much dialogue in a single story. Their characters talk on and on. This gets very boring for the reader. It's better to write a few well-written lines of dialogue than too much.

# Punctuating Dialogue

Name_____Date_____

Dialogue looks a little different than other writing. Many times young writers don't write down what their characters say because they don't know how to punctuate dialogue. These simple rules will help you learn how to write dialogue.

✓ Use quotation marks to surround spoken words.

✓ Put all punctuation marks inside the quotation marks.

✓ Indent each time someone new is speaking.

For example:

"I think it's too cold to go skating on the pond today."

"Me, too! Let's go get some hot chocolate."

"Maybe the weather will be warmer tomorrow."

If your character asks a question, use a question mark in place of a period.

"Can you come over and play video games with me today?"

Exclamation points go inside the quotation marks, too.

"We've got front row seats for the big game!"

Remember to indent when a new speaker begins speaking. Consider this example:

indent ➜ "I'm so hungry I could eat four jumbo hot dogs with ketchup, mustard, pickle relish, chili, and cheese."

indent ➜ "I could eat six. What time's lunch?"

Notice there are two speakers. The writer indented for the first speaker and indented again for the second speaker. This is the correct way to let your reader know a new person is speaking.

"Will you come over today after school?"

"Yeah, but I've got to do my homework first."

# Tagged Dialogue

Name_____Date_____

Often an author will write *he said*, *she said*, *or he asked* to let the reader know who is talking. Or, the author might use a person's name, such as, *Mario said* or *Lucy asked*. These phrases are called **dialogue tags**. Tags can appear at the beginning, ending, or even in the middle of the sentence.

"I'm going to spend the summer at the beach," he said.
Sheri said, "Not me. We're going to visit my Aunt Sue in Chicago."
"Will you take your two dogs with you?" he asked.
"No, our neighbor is going to take care of them for us," she said.

"Yo man, like, yesterday at the beach I rode the gnarliest wave that ever existed," he said. "Wish you'd been with me."
"Way cool, Dude," Tom said. "Let's go again this afternoon after school!"

"Our soccer team won big yesterday and I scored two goals," she said.
Kameko said, "Yeah, and they were a tough team to beat, too."

Tammy said, "My dad falls asleep in front of the TV every night."
"I bet he doesn't snore like my dad does," Theo said.
"Want to bet? He sounds like a freight train," Tammy said.
"My dad sounds like a fog horn," said Theo. "It's scary."

"Whoa! Look at that bruise on your arm," Marla said.
"Yeah, my skateboard hit a crack in the sidewalk and I took a bad fall yesterday after school," Adam said. "Look at my knee. No skin!"

# Punctuating Tagged Dialogue

Name_____Date_____

To punctuate tagged dialogue, add a comma between the dialogue and the speaker. Remember to use quotation marks, too.

↓

"I don't know what to do about the gorilla under my bed," he said.

If your character is asking a question, add a question mark instead of a comma.

↓

"There's a gorilla under your bed?" she asked.

If your character is excited or shouting, add an exclamation point instead of a comma.

↓

"You should see it. It's huge!" said Stan.

Practice adding the punctuation, quotation marks, and tags to the following sentences:

1. I can't go to the movies because I haven't done my homework

2. If you'd done your homework earlier you could have gone

3. Are you nagging me

4. I see flames coming from the kitchen

5. Will you be able to put out the flames or should I call 911

6. Let's go visit the new gorilla baby at the zoo.

7. What a great idea

# Dialogue With Special Tags

Name_____Date_____

Sometimes writers replace ordinary tags with special tags to give the reader more information. **Special tags are always strong verbs.** They change the meaning of the sentence. Notice the difference between ordinary tags and special tags.

"Please don't scratch your fingernails on the board again," he said.
"Please don't scratch your fingernails on the board again," he begged.

"I'm not going to eat the rest of my dinner," she said.
"I'm not going to eat the rest of my dinner," she whined.

Marvin said, "Get out of my stuff! How many times do I have to tell you?"
Marvin demanded, "Get out of my stuff! How many times do I have to tell you?"

Practice adding special tags to the following sentences:

1.    "Be careful. They might hear us,"_____ Bill.

2.    "Try saying that again to my face,"_____ Eva.

3.    "Stop, Dad. There's an injured dog on the side
      of the road,"_____ the boy.

4.    The principal _____, "Come into my office."

5.    The little girl _____, "Will I ever see my mommy again?"

6.    "Uh....I...want to....ask you something," _____Kevin.

7.    "Don't cry. Everything's going to be okay," she _____.

# Young Author's List of Special Tags

Name_____Date_____

When writing dialogue, you can mix ordinary tags such as *he said* or *she asked* with special tags. Here is a list of 99 special tags you may refer to. These words can add hidden meaning or plot clues to your writing.

| | | |
|---|---|---|
| accused | echoed | rambled |
| admitted | estimated | raved |
| agreed | exclaimed | reasoned |
| announced | explained | rebuked |
| answered | expressed | recited |
| apologized | giggled | refused |
| appealed | groaned | remarked |
| argued | guessed | repeated |
| asserted | heckled | reported |
| babbled | implored | reprimanded |
| begged | informed | responded |
| bemoaned | insinuated | retaliated |
| bickered | insisted | retorted |
| blamed | interrupted | revealed |
| bragged | invited | sassed |
| called | laughed | scolded |
| cautioned | lectured | screamed |
| charged | mentioned | shouted |
| chattered | mocked | snickered |
| claimed | mumbled | spoke |
| commented | murmured | squeaked |
| communicated | muttered | squealed |
| confided | narrated | stammered |
| confirmed | objected | stated |
| congratulated | observed | suggested |
| cried | pleaded | taunted |
| declared | pointed out | teased |
| denied | praised | thought |
| described | pronounced | uttered |
| differed | proposed | voiced |
| disagreed | protested | wondered |
| drawled | quarreled | yelled |
| droned | questioned | yelped |

# Tagless Dialogue

Name_____Date_____

Readers get bored when they have to read too many dialogue tags over and over. When only two characters are talking in your story, you might want to try tagless dialogue. **Tagless dialogue is a section of conversation that uses no tags.** The author lets the reader know who is talking by giving hints or clues in the dialogue.

Read the following section. Can you tell who is talking?

"Hey Jerry, want to go look for stuff with my metal detector?"

"I can't. Not today, anyway."

"Why not?"

"I promised my dad I'd help him paint the outside of our house."

"Can you go tomorrow?"

"Yeah, if we get finished."

"Alright, see ya."

"Bye, Carla."

You could tell by the dialogue there are two kids speaking. The author gives us clues so we can keep the characters straight. We don't need to keep reading *he said* or *said Jerry*. Tagless dialogue sounds very real, almost like you're eavesdropping on someone's conversation. It's a good technique to use, if done properly.

Use the space below to write a tagless dialogue conversation between two kids paddling a canoe together. Limit yourself to four to six lines of dialogue.

# Understanding Writing Prompts

Name_____Date_____

Writing about your feelings and interests is what becoming an author is all about. Every kid should have plenty of opportunities to write about things he likes. However, while you're learning basic writing skills at school, sometimes you might be asked to write to a prompt. **A prompt guides you to a specific story or topic.**

A **writing prompt** can be anything from a **subject** or **topic** to a **story-starter.** It's designed to get your creative juices flowing. Sometimes an entire class writes to the same prompt. This way, you and your fellow writers can compare your writing, supporting details, or how you each ended your stories. Learning from one another is a great way to improve your author skills and learn how a variety of writers think.

## Fictional Narrative Prompts

**A fictional narrative prompt asks you to tell an imaginative story that has a problem and a solution.** A fictional narrative prompt might look like this story-starter:

You are spending the day at the beach with your friends. While you are digging through wet sand to build a sand castle, you find a small, golden box. Light radiates from inside. The box begins to vibrate in your hand. You are absolutely astonished, but that's nothing compared with what happens next....

**As with all narratives, a fictional narrative shows the passing of time.** It can be completely made-up or an imaginative account of something that really happened, such as a historical event. **Fictional narrative clues are words like *Imagine, What happens next?, Make-believe, Pretend, Create,* or, *Write the ending of the story.***

When you read a writing prompt, study it carefully. To determine if it is a fictional narrative prompt, ask yourself the following questions:

1. Does this prompt ask me to make up a story out of my imagination?

2. Can I create characters, situations, and dialogue that never really happened?

If the answer is yes, the prompt is a ficitonal narrative prompt.

Understanding Writing Prompts...continued

# Personal Narrative Prompts

**A personal narrative prompt asks you to tell about something that has really happened to you personally.** Although a personal narrative involves the passing of time,  it does not necessarily have to have a problem and a solution. Personal narratives combine elements of both story-telling and expository writing.

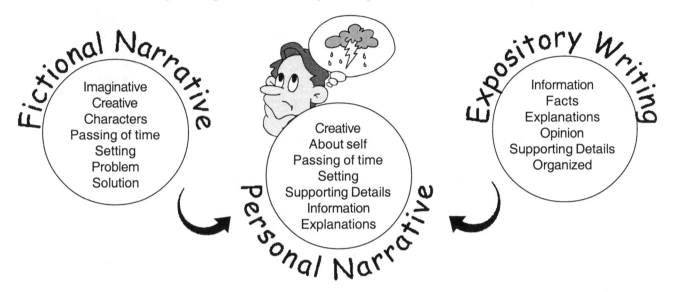

Here is an example of a personal narrative prompt:

Tell about a time when you did something that made you feel very proud of yourself.

**Personal Narrative clue words are *Tell about the time, Write about a time when*, or, *Tell what happened when you were...***

# Expository Writing Prompts

An **expository prompt** doesn't direct you to write a story. Instead, **an expository prompt asks you to write about a specific *subject*.** For instance:

Large, wild animals have intrigued mankind for thousands of years. Which wild animal do you find the most fascinating, and why?

**Expository prompts ask you for information, directions, opinions, or to persuade the reader. Expository prompt clues are words like *Explain, Convince, Why, Give reasons*, or, *How do you....?***

# Recognizing Writing Prompts

Name_____Date_____

It's important for writers to be able to tell the difference between different kinds of writing prompts. Read the prompts below as a class. Discuss what each prompt asks you to write. Write **FN** for **fictional narrative prompts, PN** for **personal narrative prompts, and E for expository prompts**.

1. _____ Explain why athletes have to have special training.

2. _____ What is your favorite restaurant, and why?

3. _____ Tell about a time when someone made you very angry.

4. _____ Explain how to make your favorite after school snack.

5. _____ While pulling weeds, you find a gold ring in your backyard. You notice the ring glows in the dark. Tell what happens when you put the mysterious ring on your finger.

6. _____ In your opinion, what animal would be the least desirable to have as a pet?

7. _____ You come home to find your parents sitting in a limo in front of your house. Write the story of what happens next.

8. _____ Convince the class that we should have 30 minutes of free time each day to talk to kids from other classes.

9. _____ You find an unusual book in a trunk of your grandmother's attic. It is a storybook for kids. When you open the pages, the characters in the pictures come alive and invite you into the story. What happens next?

10. _____ How do you help the rest of the members of your family?

11. _____ What reasons could you give to support the statement, "Kids should be allowed to have a job and earn money?"

12. _____ Tell about a time when you did something you weren't supposed to do and had to learn a hard lesson.

# Addressing a Prompt

Name_____Date_____

Kids sometimes make a BIG mistake when they start writing without addressing the prompt. It leads to a lot of confusion! The reader has no clue as to what their topic is. **Addressing the prompt means talking about the topic right away so your reader will know what you are writing about.** Let's imagine this is the expository writing prompt:

### What is one chore you've done lately that you've been dreading for a long time?

Instead of addressing the prompt and letting the reader know what she's going to write about, the author just jumps into the details of the dreaded chore:

He needed a bath, so I filled the tub with warm, sudsy water. Next, I got out some towels and a huge bar of soap. This wasn't going to be easy!

Who needed a bath? Her little brother? A stray cat? A sick chimpanzee? The writer didn't tell us, so we are left to wonder. It is better to let the reader know what you're talking about by addressing the prompt right away.

My dog Bentley has needed a bath for days, but I kept putting it off because he is so stinky! Last night, I filled the tub with warm, sudsy water. Next, I got out some towels and a huge bar of soap. This wasn't going to be easy!

Now, that makes more sense. Don't write any details until you've let the reader know what you are talking about. Don't write out the entire prompt or repeat it word for word. Address the prompt by giving the reader clues or telling him what you're writing about. Here's a fictional narrative prompt:

### You and your class are camping in the woods on a field trip. Tell what happens when you wander off by yourself and get lost in the woods.

The first sentence should talk about the prompt but not repeat it word for word.

### After five hours of trying to make my way back through the woods to the others, I had to face the ugly truth: I was lost.

# Can You Address a Prompt?

Name_____Date_____

**When writing to a prompt, the very first sentence should tell the reader what you're writing about.** It's not a good thing to copy the entire prompt as a beginning. However, it is a good thing to mention the important parts of the prompt in the first sentence.

Read the prompts below. Practice writing first sentences that refer to the main ideas of each prompt. Everyone's sentences will be different. Compare sentences and share good ideas and techniques.

1     Fictional Narrative Prompt: **You and your friends are shopping in an unfamiliar part of town. As you wander in and out of the shops and stores, a sign on a street corner catches your eye. It says, "Free Trip in Time Machine." An old gentleman is standing next to a homemade contraption that has gadgets and knobs on the outside. He is inviting the crowd to take a time-trip. Tell what happens next....**

2     Fictional Narrative Prompt: **The year is 1912. The ship is the RMS Titanic. The time is the middle of the night. You are awakened by a loud knock on your door. "Put on your life vests," a voice calls. You rush into the hall to see what's happening. Write the ending of the story.**

3     Personal Narrative Prompt: **What is one of your favorite memories from your childhood?**

4     Personal Narrative Prompt: **Tell about a time when you forgot to do something important.**

5     Expository Prompt: **Getting along with other people leads to friendships. How important are friendships, and what are some things you can do to be a good friend to someone else?**

6     Expository Prompt: **Moms always seem to be nagging kids to clean their rooms. Do you think kids should have to keep their rooms clean, or should they be allowed to keep their rooms any way they want to?**

# Temporary Spelling

Name_____Date_____

It would be great if kids knew how to spell every word they wanted to use, but most kids don't. They often have to use a dictionary, spelling list, word wall, or ask a teacher for help. When you are writing your rough drafts, don't take the time to stop and look up a particular word. You can do that later during the editing process. For the time being, use temporary spelling.

**Temporary spelling means guessing how a word is spelled.** Think about the word you want to use, and listen to the way it sounds in your head. Spell it like it sounds or put down a few letters so you can remember what word you meant later on. Continue writing your narrative or expository piece. Later you can "fix" the temporary spelling by looking up the correct spelling of the words you guessed at. Cross out the word, insert a proofreader's caret, and write the correct spelling up above the temporary spelling. Easy.

imagine

Can you imajn living in a country that is at war

Ireland Bosnia

all the time? In countries like Eyerland, Boznee, and

bombs

Afghanistan

Afg millions of kids have to live in fear of boms,

snipers, guns, tanks, and military guys. They get post

traumatic syndrome          nervous condition

tr stress sindr and that's a terrible nervus condishin.

Correcting the spelling helps you learn the proper way to spell the words you guessed at. Rough drafts can have temporary spelling. However, if you're going to publish your piece, try to use good spelling so your reader won't trip over your words.

# Jotting

Name_____Date_____

The human brain is an amazing computer. When we concentrate and brainstorm ideas, it's like explosions, bells, whistles, and sirens going off in our brains all at once. We think much faster than we can write down words and sentences. Writing down your ideas quickly, before they disappear, is tough. Jotting can help you do this. **Jotting means writing down a few letters of a word.**

ele = elephant          fav = favorite          nt = night time

**Jotting also means drawing a very simple picture that stands for what you want to write down.**

= cloud          = ocean          = sunshine

When your brain is really sizzling with ideas, writing down every word or sentence would slow you down. Instead, "jot" down a couple of letters or draw a very simple picture. This is not the time for fancy artwork or illustrations. Just a few lines of a picture to record your idea is better.

Let's pretend you are asked to write about an elephant you see on your field trip to the local zoo. Your brain remembers many details about the elephant, what it looks like, what it smells like, what it sounds like. You want to get these thoughts down as quickly as possible so you don't forget them. If you try to write them out completely, you get bogged down by spelling and the time it takes to write each word. Your brain has to slow down to the speed of your hand. It might take you many minutes to write out these thoughts and words, especially if you are concerned with perfect spelling:

big ears, enormous, little eyes, gray skin, little tail,

coarse hairs on skin, large toenails, ivory tusks

Nothing is *wrong* with writing down each word during brainstorming. It's just that it *takes too long*. There's a better way to record your thoughts when you're trying to recall details and generate ideas. **Jotting helps you to get your thoughts down as quicky as possible without worrying about spelling or perfection.**

## Jotting...continued

Jotting looks weird and even silly, because you're writing just a few letters that stand for words and drawing simple pictures to remind you of certain details. Here's an example of jotting down ideas about the same elephant with the "translations" included so you can know what the letters and drawings stand for.

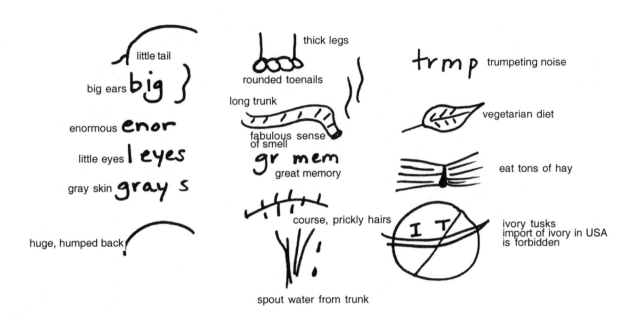

The spelling is primitive. The drawings are **simple**, but the author recorded 18 important ideas in the same time it would take her to write out five to ten. What a great leap of progress for young writers!

If you're not going to write a story or piece about your jotted topic right away, it's a good idea to transcribe the list. You can do this at school or later, at home. **Transcribing means taking the time to write down the word or thought represented by each jot.** That way, you won't forget what that silly-looking squiggle or those weird letters mean.

Adults use jotting all the time to take down directions, recipes, or phone messages. They do it because it's quick and easy. They don't want to waste their valuable time writing things out when just a few letters, pictures, or abbreviations will do.

With just a little practice, jotting can become your new best friend. Don't get hung up on spelling or neatness. You'll have time later to go back and translate your jotting and correct the spelling if you need to. Jotting is only temporary. Authors use jotting to record ideas that come into their brains faster than their hands can write.

 Remember: Jotting is a temporary tool that helps us record ideas faster.

# Practicing Jotting

Name_____Date_____

The more you practice jotting, the easier it becomes. Try this practice exercise. The subject is: **things in your bedroom**. Jot specific details with a few letters, words, or quick, simple drawings. Try to get as many ideas down as you can in five minutes.

# Target Skills in Children's Literature

## Dialogue
Sachar, Louis. *Wayside School is Falling Down*. New York: Avon, 1989.
Spinelli, Jerry. *Fourth Grade Rats*. New York: Scholastic, 1991.

## Descriptive Writing
Crane, Carol. *S is for Sunshine*. Chelsea: Sleeping Bear Press, 2000.
Simms, Laura. *Rotten Teeth*. New York: Houghton Mifflin, 1998.
Smith, Dodie. *The 101 Dalmations*. New York: Puffin, 1956.
Talbot, Hudson. *O'Sullivan Stew*. New York: G.P. Putnam's Sons, 1999.
Tanaka, Shelley. *On Board the Titanic*. New York: Heperion Books for Children, 1997.

## Juicy Color Words
Hamanaka, Seila. *All the Colors of the Earth*. New York: Morrow Jr. Books, 1994.
O'Neill, Mary. *Hailstones & Halibut Bones*. New York: Doubleday, 1989.
McMillan, Bruce. *Growing Colors*. New York: Lothrop, Lee and Shepard Books, 1988.

## Onomatopoeia
Fleischman, Paul. *Joyful Noise: Poems for Two Voices*. New York: Harper, 1988.
Gray, Libba Moore. *Mama Had a Dancing Heart*. New York: Orchard, 1995.
Hesse, Karen. *The Music of Dolphins*. New York: Scholastic, 1996.
Martin, Bill Jr. and John Archambault. *Chicka Chicka Boom Boom*. New York: Simon & Schuster, 1989.
Root, Phyllis. *What Baby Wants*. Cambridge: Candlewick, 1998.

## Similes and Metaphors
O'Dell, Scott. *Island of the Blue Dolphins*. New York: Dell, 1960.
Paulsen, Gary. *The Cookcamp*. New York: Dell, 1991.
Voigt, Cynthia. *The Vandemark Mummy*. New York: Fawcet Junier, 1991.

## Specific Emotion Words
DiCamillo, Kate. *Because of Winn Dixie*. Cambridge: Candlewick, 2000.
Fox, Paula. *Slave Dancer*. Scarsdale: Bradbury Press, 1973.
Holm, Jennifer. *Our Only May Amelia*. New York: Harper Collins, 1999.
Joseph, Lynn. *The Color of My Words*. New York: Joanna Cotler Books, 2000.
Munsch, Robert. *Love You Forever*. Buffalo: Firefly Books, Ltd, 1986.
Naylor, Phillis Reynolds. *Shiloh*. New York: Maxwell MacMillan, 1991.
Richardson, Arleta. *Looking for Home*. Elgin: Chariot, 1993.

## Strong Verbs
Allen, Valerie. *The Night Thief*. Gretna: Pelican, 1990.
Dahl, Roald. *Charlie and the Chocolate Factory*. New York: Knopf, 1964.
Hartmann, Jack. *Over in the Ocean*. St. Petersburg: Hop 2 It Press, 1999.
Vaughan, Marcia. *The Secret to Freedom*. New York: Lee & Low Books, 2001.

## Transition Words and Phrases
O'Dell, Scott. *Sing Down the Moon*. New York: Dell, 1970.
Robinson, Barbara. *My Brother Louis Measures Worms*. New York: Harper, 1988.
Warren, Andrea. *Orphan Train Rider*. Boston: Houghton Mifflin, 1996.

# NOTES

# Fictional Narratives

# Fictional Narratives

Name_____Date_____

Don't you just love a good story? Life would be pretty boring without fire-breathing dragons, aliens that land on the school playground, crazy inventors, and brave heroes who ride off into battle. Consider some of the classic children's stories:

Little Red Riding Hood
The Three Little Pigs
Charlotte's Web
Peter Pan
The Lion King
Green Eggs and Ham
Jack and the Beanstalk
Charlie and the Chocolate Factory

You probably know hundreds of other stories, too, and have written some yourself. Another word for story is *narrative.* That's the fancy name we sometimes use at school. Whenever you hear the word narrative, **it usually means either a made-up story, called a fictional narrative,** or, **something that has happened to you, called a personal narrative.** Both fictional narratives and personal narratives show the passing of time.

Right now let's focus on **fictional narratives**. These are stories we make up out of our own imagination. Fictional narratives usually have a **main character, other minor characters, a problem or challenge for the main character to face, a setting, time frame, solution,** and **takeaway.**

You might write a story about an imaginary girl who catches a magic fish and is granted three wishes. You might also write tall tales, science fiction, folk tales, mysteries, adventures, or a fictionalized account of an event in history or a real person's life.

In our real lives, we're told never to tell a lie. As a matter of fact, telling lies can get us into all sorts of trouble. But when you're a writer working on a story, you are allowed to make stuff up. Use your imagination. Be creative. Write about wild, exotic things you could only dream about. Create a wonderful world of make-believe. Put your characters in scary or humorous situations that will entertain your readers or tickle their funny bones.

Take Dr. Seuss, for example. We know that he didn't really eat green eggs and ham or run the circus, or have a crazy cat who wore a hat. Those are just stories he made up to entertain millions of kids and adults. As you read fictional narratives, ask yourself some key questions: What makes this piece enjoyable? How does the writer create a fantasy world? How can I use some of these techniques to enhance my own fiction?

# Fictional Narrative Example

Name_____Date_____

## The Laundry Closet Door          by a 4th grade student

The nightmare started on a dreary, rainy Saturday afternoon. Mom was out on a date with my dad. I was lounging on the couch at home, watching a boring movie that my dad had rented for me. My eyes began to droop.

Suddenly, my eyes flew open! I'd heard a sound, a low, moaning sound. It sounded like it was coming from the downstairs laundry closet. Mom's daily warning raced through my head, "Never, ever go down into the laundry room closet!" But my curiosity overwhelmed my conscience. I silently turned off the TV and hesitantly made my way to the laundry closet. My palms were sweating as I got closer and closer to the moaning.

"I'm not afraid.....I'm not a-a-afraid," I was constantly thinking. I finally got to the laundry closet door. Chattering teeth, sweating palms and all, I reached for the cold metal door handle. I hesitated, then opened the door. The disgusting smell of sewage water mixed with dead carcasses wafted to my nostrils.

"Oh, boy, now look what you got yourself into," I thought. Stepping over puddles and muck, I made my way to what looked like a staircase. As I touched the slimy railing and stepped down onto the first step, SLAM! The laundry closet door slammed behind me! This wasn't good.

"You've come this far," I told myself, "You might as well go all the way."

Stepping nervously from step to step, I made my way towards the bottom of the staircase. After what seemed like hours of listening to the moaning getting louder and louder, closer and closer, I finally came to the bottom.

Then I stepped into a room that was about the size of my living room. The noise stopped. Ancient torches cast a very dim light and cobwebs reached out to touch my face like dirty hands. In the very middle of the cold stone room was a long, narrow chest. Foreign writing and inscriptions decorated the four sides and top.

I shakily, cautiously, nervously stepped up to the chest. The chest had no bolt on it. I figured it wasn't treasure. Wiping the dust off the top, I said, "Here goes nothing!" and gently lifted the chest top open. There, hands folded over the chest, mouth in a wide grin, lay the carcass of my deceased great-great-grandmother!

"Aaaaghaaaaaaaagh!!!!" I ran screaming from the room, up the stairs three at a time, out of the closet, and, slamming the door shut behind me, fled into the safety of my room. I bolted the door behind me.

About an hour or two later, I was lying on my bed, calmly reading a book, when Mom knocked on the door. "Did you have a good time?" she wondered.

"Uh..." I would never tell her the truth. "...Yeah."

"Good." She walked away, leaving me to my thoughts. Never in my life will I ever go down there again. Oh, and remember, if you don't want to see a horrifying sight, don't ever go near the laundry closet door.

# Fictional Narrative Writing Prompts

Name_____Date_____

Telling and writing good fiction stories are very helpful skills. Try your hand at these.

**1** You are in your classroom one morning when the school principal's voice comes over the intercom and calls you to the office. Your parents are waiting for you, smiling. The principal points outside to a long white limousine parked in front of the school. "Someone is here to see you," she says. You look at your parents, and they nod their approval. You walk out to the limousine, wondering who is inside. With a whirr, the dark-tinted window rolls down....

**2** You receive a package from your pen-pal in India. After opening it, you are quite disappointed to discover a dusty old rug inside. When you shake out the dust to have a better look at the rug, you discover that it is really a magic carpet. There is a message pinned to one edge of the carpet....

**3** The President of the United States has issused an open invitation for eight kids to live inside the International Space Station in outer space for one month. Along with a special teacher and seven other kids, you have been chosen. You've been through the pre-training, said good-bye to your friends, and now the day is here....

**4** On your way home from school, you pass an old woman selling something. She has a sign that reads, "Magic Cookies, 25 cents." You have two quarters, so you think, *why not?*....

Fictional Prompts...continued

While digging with a shovel around the roots of a big tree in your back yard, you hear a *clink*. Scraping deeper, your shovel hits something solid and metallic. You discover an ancient metal box with some writing on the top. Using a small trowel, you scrape until the box is free. Your fingers tremble as you lift the lid....

Ah, the perfect afternoon...looking for shells along the seashore. While searching at the water's edge, you notice something bobbing and floating in the gentle waves: a glass bottle. The mouth of the bottle has been sealed with wax. Your heart begins to beat faster when you notice a rolled-up, paper note inside....

You and your friends have tickets for the circus. At the door, the ringmaster calls you over. "Hey, Kid," he says. "The guy we we normally shoot out of the cannon is too sick to perform tonight. He's about your size. I'll give you $1,000 if you'll take his place for just one show." All you can think about is earning $1,000 for one circus performance....

Could the treasure map you find in an old trunk be real? Probably not, but, since it leads to an abandoned cave not too far away, you and your friends decide to check it out. You pack a picnic lunch, grab your flashlights, and set out on your bikes. You and your friends have no idea of the life-changing adventure that awaits you in the secret cave....

# Story Glove

Name_____Date_____

There are formulas for chemical experiments, rocket fuel, and even miracle drugs that cure exotic diseases. Did you know there is also a formula for writing a good story? It's called the **Story Glove** and it's easy to follow. It works especially well when you are given a **prompt, or story starter.**

The palm of the glove is the **prompt**. You can write your prompt on a sticky note and stick it in the palm of the glove to help you focus on the topic. Just like all the fingers of a glove can touch the palm of the glove, all the points of a story focus on the **prompt.** The thumb is the **grabber**. Always try to start your story by "hooking" the reader. The index finger is the **problem or challenge**. Something good or bad has to happen to the main character to propel the story forward. The middle finger is the **action of the story**.

This is the main part of the story where you tell the readers how the problem or challenge affects the main character. Be sure to give lots of details in the action of the story. The ring finger is the **solution**. This is where you solve the problem or overcome the challenge. The solution should be very satisfying for the reader. The little finger, or "pinkie," is the **takeaway**. The takeaway is what the main character learns or how his life changes. The takeaway is only one or two sentences long.

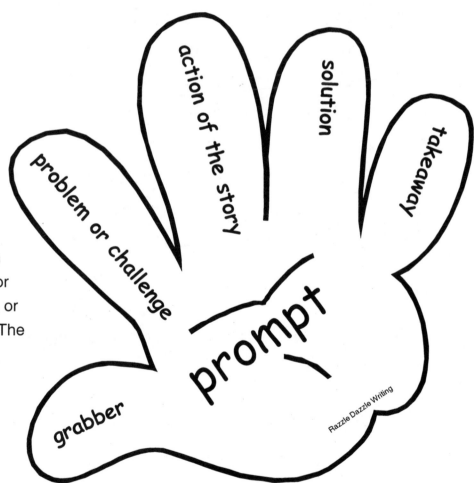

Glue an extra copy of the Story Glove to a piece of cardboard or a manila folder. Cut out the glove carefully and fasten it to the end of a popsicle stick or thin, wooden dowel. Keep the **Story Glove** handy when you are writing to help you remember the formula for great stories from prompts.

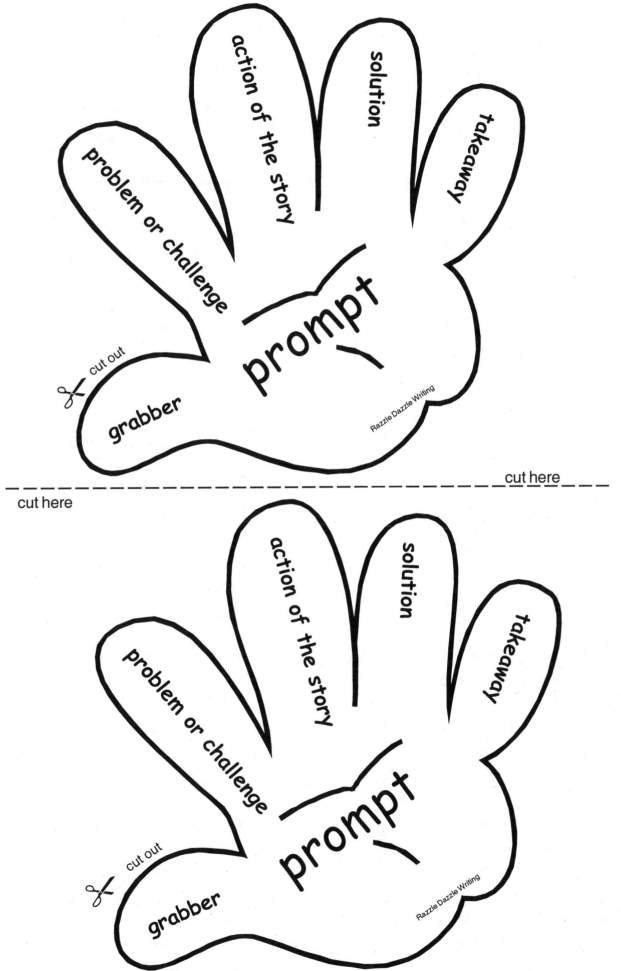

# Narrative Grabbers

Name_____ Date_____

Hmmmm...Let's see now.... When you're writing a story, what's the best way to get your reader's attention right away? Many professional writers start off with a sentence that "hooks" the reader. **This curiosity-stirring sentence is called a *grabber*.**

**Grabbers catch our attention right at the beginning and make us want to read the rest of the story.**

Some stories start with ordinary sentences that don't really "tickle" our curiosity.

Once upon a time there was a little girl.
Jack lived with his mother.
The little dog was brown.

These sentences are okay, but they don't really capture our attention. Grabbers, on the other hand, use words that make us want to keep reading to see what happens next.

**Sally Romano was a ten-year-old girl who lived all alone in an empty house by the sea.**

**"Mother," called Jack, "The three beans have grown into a magical beanstalk that leads up to the sky!"**

**The little brown dog limped through town, dragging one bloody paw behind him.**

Grabbers should make the reader feel **curiosity, humor, wonder, sympathy, anger, sorrow, fear,** or **mystery.** These feelings cause the reader to want to know what happens next. They get hooked on your story! There are many different types of grabbers:

| | |
|---|---|
| Mystery Statement | I was eleven when I found the magic key that would change my life. |
| Shocking Statement | I'll never forget the day my tongue turned purple and green. |
| Humorous Statement | I didn't mean to drive my teacher crazy, it just happened that way. |
| Onomatopoeia | Crash! I knew I was in trouble as soon as I heard that sound. |
| Dialogue | "Why are you eating a tarantula?" my little sister asked. |
| Rhetorical Question | Don't you think every boy deserves to have a dog of his own? |

# Choosing the Grabbers

Name_____Date_____

Writers often build a following of readers by "hooking" their attention right away with great grabbers. Read the sentences below. If one grabs your attention, or rouses your curiosity, **mark it G for grabber**. If the sentence is ordinary or boring, **mark it O**.

1. _____ Bird Dog Dean hadn't planned to set the woods on fire.

2. _____ Jimmy wanted to be a fireman when he grew up.

3. _____ Sasha scrounged through the garbage can because she hadn't eaten in two days.

4. _____ When Mom told me Michael Jordan was on the phone for me, I couldn't believe my ears!

5. _____ Everyone thought the injured dog should be put to sleep, except me.

6. _____ Once upon a time, there lived an old woman and an old man.

7. _____ My best friend's name is Lee Ann Turwilliger.

8. _____ "Look at this little beauty," the Crocodile Hunter, Steve Irwin, said to me as we trekked through the jungle together.

9. _____ This is a story about a moose I saw once in Maine.

10. _____ I've never told this story before, and I'm only telling it now because I think someone else should know the truth.

11. _____ How was I supposed to know that Marty Hopper was going to get me in trouble?

12. _____ It was my turn to bathe the dog.

13. _____ "Shark!" Dad screamed. "Get out of the water!"

14. _____ My family and I went to the movies last Saturday afternoon.

15. _____ It all happened when I was eight years old.

16. _____ In case you're thinking of buying a 20-foot long python for a pet, I have one word for you: *don't.*

# Young Author's Narrative Grabber Collection

Name_____Date_____

Collecting grabbers from professional writers is a good way to learn how to write them yourself. Search for grabbers in books, magazine articles, and short stories. Write the very best ones you find here for a ready reference. When you start a new story, check your grabber list for innovative ideas. Change the grabber to fit your story, and you're off!

## Great Grabbers!

Remember: The purpose of a grabber is to capture the reader's attention at the beginning of the piece.

# Problem or Challenge

Name_____Date_____

Most fictional narratives have a **problem** or **challenge** that leads to some action. The problem or challenge makes the reader want to know how the story turns out.

This is especially true when you're flipping through the television channels. Flip... flip...flip...Nothing really interesting....On the next channel you see a rabbit being chased by a rattlesnake. You stay on that channel just to see what finally happens. Does the rattlesnake have rabbit burgers for lunch? Does the bunny escape?

Next, you flip to another channel and see a competition between kids racing to the top of a hill to win a big reward. Who will win? Will it be a close race?

**A problem is a negative situation.** Something goes wrong. Something terrible happens. The main character finds himself in a bad situation he doesn't want to be in.

A grizzly bear wanders into the campsite
    where you and your friends are sleeping....

Nancy accidentally mixes in soap flakes instead of the powdered
    sugar for the cake she is baking for the 4-H contest....

The boat Esmeralda and Wendy are paddling through the swamp
    hits a stump and springs a leak. An alligator is approaching....

**A challenge is a positive situation.** A competition. A contest. An adventure. The main character must prove something or wants to accomplish something.

Dale is trying to sell lemonade to earn enough
    money to buy the little dog in the pet
    store window before someone else buys him....

Nguyen has entered the Jr. Olympics and wants to win
    a gold medal in the boys' archery contest....

Tyrell got a new metal detector for his birthday and he wants to
    look for buried treasure in the field behind his house....

# Problems and Challenges Create Tension

Name_____Date_____

Thinking up a problem or challenge for her main character is one of the toughest things an author has to do. **The problem or challenge causes tension or conflict.** Without an interesting or exciting problem or challenge, there isn't much of a story.

**Authors have to think creatively.** This takes practice. The more you do it, the easier it becomes when you want to write a story other people will want to read. Make sure your problem or challenge is something other kids will think is interesting or exciting. For instance, if you were writing about two best friends, they could....

...try camping out in the back yard for the first time.

...accidentally set the shed on fire while trying to light some fireworks.

...break a neighbor's window while playing baseball.

...enter the skateboard competition at the park.

...take horseback riding lessons together.

...sneak into the basement of the town museum to see some secret dinosaur bones.

...find a bag of stolen jewelry buried under an old tree.

...have to take care of a baby elephant for the weekend.

The only limit is your own imagination. When you're writing a story, anything can happen! Kids like to read stories about other kids who:

| | |
|---|---|
| have a magical or fantastic experience | have to do something scary |
| have to solve a problem without an adult's help | get into trouble |
| have a special relationship with an animal | face danger |
| get to do something kids don't usually get to do | solve a mystery |
| try creative ways to make money | rescue a friend or animal |
| go somewhere interesting or special | do something silly or stupid |
| want to win a contest | want someone to like them |

# Creating Story Problems and Challenges

Name_____Date_____

In fictional narratives, having the main character face a problem or challenge always makes things more interesting.

Characters: Two best friends
Setting: They are home alone in the afternoon
Problems: They decide to dye each other's hair a wild color....
They try on the mother's jewelry and accidentally drop her special ring down through the floor vent....

Challenges: They decide to build a really neat clubhouse....
They want to create a winning science project....

Make up and write five more problems or challenges that could happen to two best friends. Think of things that are scary, funny, silly, crazy, adventurous, or dangerous. What *could happen* to two best friends home alone in the afternoon?

1 _____

2 _____

3 _____

4 _____

5 _____

Exchange papers with two or three other writers and compare your problems and challenges with theirs. Ask each writer to put a star by the problem he thinks is your very best one. Help each other get new ideas for problems and improve your old ones.

# Settings, Problems, and Challenges

Name_____Date_____

**The location in which a story takes place is called the *setting*.** Where you set your story gives it a certain feel, or mood. For instance, a story set in the wilderness of Alaska has a different feel to it than a story set down in a ruby mine in North Carolina. Interesting or unusual settings create a "stage" for your characters. Invent three different problems or challenges that would be fun to write about for each of the following settings.

On a camping trip

1 _____

2 _____

3 _____

At the zoo

1 _____

2 _____

3 _____

At a summer camp

1 _____

2 _____

3 _____

In the jungle

1 _____

2 _____

3 _____

# Lights, Camera, ACTION!

Name_____Date_____

Did you ever read a book that never seemed to go anywhere? It's hard to make yourself read to the end. Without action, you don't have much of a story.

Giving your main characters a problem or challenge sets up the action, or plot, of the story. When readers know something might go wrong, or there's a challenge to face, they want to read further to see what happens. In other words, they are interested in the **action of the story.**

A good writer gives the reader plenty of action.

LIGHTS! CAMERA! ACTION!

Will the main character win the race?
Does the hero die?
Will the kids get in trouble?
Does the bad guy get caught?
What happens next?

The answers to these questions keep the reader interested until the very last page. As a matter of fact, sometimes readers get so excited they can't wait until the ending. They peek ahead to see what's going to happen.

Think of it this way. Imagine it's the Fourth of July. You're having a big family get-together by a beautiful lake: boating, picnicing, swimming, the works. All the kids are looking forward to setting off the big collection of fireworks your Uncle Harry has brought. As it gets dark, however, the adults sit around talking. You keep looking hopefully at the fireworks stash, but no one does anything. *But what about the bottle rockets,* you think. *Where are the firecrackers? Have we waited all this time for nothing?* You want something to happen. You want ACTION.

Think of a good book you've read recently or one your class has read together. What are some things that happened in the action part of the story? Ask yourself these thought-provoking questions:

What were some major events that happened in the story?
Why did these events keep you wanting to read the rest of the story?
How does action build excitement for the reader?
How can you, as a writer, keep your readers wanting more?

# Creating Story Action

Name_____Date_____

**Story action keeps the reader turning the pages to see what will happen next.**
This is where writers have to use their imaginations. Don't be too predictable. Stay away from
what you've read dozens of times before. Try to create new, exciting things to happen to your
main character. Write nerve-wracking, suspense-building, rib-tickling, or spine-tingling action
that will thrill your readers. For instance, imagine the following scene:

**Main character:**  An ordinary kid

**Setting:**  The principal's office

**Problem:**  The kid has been sent to the office for being late too many times.

**Action:**  The principal has to leave his office for a few minutes and asks the kid
to stay seated and wait for him. While the principal is out of the room,
the kid spots a bag of marbles up high on one of the shelves. It's the
same marble bag the principal took away from the kid's best friend.
The kid climbs on a chair and stretches up to get the marbles back
so he can be a hero and return them to his friend. He reaches the
bag of marbles, but it tips over and marbles spill out all over the floor.
The principal opens the door just at this moment and sees the kid up
on the chair holding the empty bag. He steps on a marble, loses his
balance, and lands flat on his back. The chair begins to topple, the
kid flies through the air and lands on top of the principal.

Get the picture? The action builds on the problem. In this scene, the kid was already in
trouble for being late too many times. We know he should have stayed seated and waited for
the principal to return. But readers love action. They secretly want something to happen that
will make them laugh, or cringe, or be scared out of their wits. So, the writer of the story has
to write something creative that will thrill the reader. That is his responsibility.

How do writers do this? Put yourself in the story. When you're alone in someone's
office, aren't you tempted to snoop around? This kid sees his friend's bag of marbles. Even
though it's wrong, he wants to swipe the marbles back so he can brag about it to his friends.
Of course, just at the moment he gets the bag in his hands, the worst happens! They spill out.
The reader is very nervous at this point, because he knows the kid will probably get caught.
The writer makes it even worse by having the principal slip on a marble and fall. This is funny
for kids to visualize. The big "whammy" is having the kid fall on the principal. Horrors!

# Creating Satisfying Solutions

Name_____Date_____

Have you ever read a great story that was exciting and kept your interest but then ended too suddenly? You might have felt let-down or cheated. The ending wasn't satisfying. Some questions were left unanswered. The writer left you hanging. This is a big no-no!

Consider this story snippet, for example:

**Main Character:** a 5th grade student named Tad

**Setting:** an alien spacecraft

**Problem:** Tad got onto the spacecraft when it landed in his backyard but did not get off before it left Earth. He has been trapped on board.

**Action:** The large, bug-eyed alien slowly lumbered towards him. Its yellow fangs were bared, and its mouth was drooling. "Please don't eat me," Tad pleaded. His heart pounded in his chest, and he wanted to run away, but his feet felt like lead weights. "This is it," he thought. "I'm going to be lunch meat for some hideous looking alien." Tad prepared to die.

At this point, we want to know what happens to Tad and the alien. We'd feel terribly let down if we had to read one of these lame endings for a solution:

I hope you liked my story.
That's all there is to my story.
And they all lived happily, ever-after.
Then Tad woke up and realized that it was all a dream.

Instead, we want to read a **solution that solves the problem and satisfies the reader.** Here is one ending possibility that does just that:

Tad noticed that one of the alien's fangs was as black as charcoal and full of holes. In desperation, he gripped the fang with both hands and wrenched with all his might. The alien screamed in pain and grabbed his jaw. There was a loud *snap.* To Tad's amazement, the alien stopped yelling and slowly began to smile. "That tooth has been hurting me for the last trillion miles or so," he said. "You have relieved my pain. If you wish, I will return you to the Earth-planet to show my gratitude."

And so, after the long ride back from outer space to his own backyard, Tad waved good-bye to the alien. As the spacecraft soared out of sight, Tad realized he was still clutching the alien's fang. My friends might not believe me, Tad thought, but this fang is all the proof I need. This is one adventure I'll never forget.

# Takeaway Endings

Name_____ Date _____

When you begin writing a story, it's good to capture the reader's attention right away. But did you know the way we *end* a piece of writing is as important as the way we start one? A good writer sums up his narrative story with a great ending, sometimes called a takeaway. **A takeaway is one or two sentences that tell the reader what the main character learned, or how his life has changed.**

For example:

"I'll never forget this place as long as I live," Addie said. "Things change," she thought. "Change isn't so bad after all."

Another example:

As Buddy said good-bye to his friends he realized that this summer at Camp Kippy was one of the best summers of his life.

You've seen **takeaways** at the end of television programs such as *The Waltons*, *The Wonder Years*, or *Anne of Green Gables*. You've seen them at the end of movies like *Home Alone* or *Indiana Jones and the Last Crusade*. You've read takeaway endings at the end of favorite chapter books and stories. They're everywhere!

The short story below is about a dog who runs away from home and gets into trouble. Notice how the takeaway ending tells how Buddy's life has changed.

Buddy lived in the backyard behind Pete's house. One day, when Pete left for school, Buddy dug a hole under the fence and crawled under. He had never been out in the neighborhood without Pete before. I'll explore, Buddy thought, and off he went, running wild.

When Buddy tried to cross the street to get to the park, a car had to screech to a stop, almost hitting the little dog. In the park, he ran into a couple of mean boys who yelled and threw rocks at him. After a while, it started to rain, and Buddy was soaked to the skin. I miss Pete, he thought. His ears dripped and his tail drooped.

Buddy walked home in the rain, dripping wet and lonely. Why had he gone out without his friend, Pete? Just as Buddy arrived home, Pete got off the school bus. "What are you doing out of the fence?" Pete asked. He hugged his little dog. Buddy wagged his tail furiously.

An adventure is best, Buddy thought, when you can share it with a friend like Pete.

# Examples of Takeaway Endings

Name_____Date_____

Takeaway endings are little "diamonds" that tell us what the main character learned, or how his life changed. Here are some examples of takeaway endings for you to refer to:

1.    My close call with a giant alligator has certainly taught me not to dangle my feet in the water while canoeing.

2.    After spending that cold, lonely night in the woods, I'll never disobey my father's warnings again.

3.    Getting that little puppy for my birthday has changed my life. I now have a lifelong friend who loves me, just for being me.

4.    You can be sure that I won't be playing around lawn mowers after my long day in the Emergency Room.

5.    Watching TV is okay, but reading a good mystery really gets my heart pumping.

6.    You better be careful the next time you're tempted to sneak outside at night. You might run into trouble!

7.    Uncle Henry taught me more about playing checkers in one afternoon than I had learned my entire life. I hope that when I grow up I can teach my own nephew how to play championship checkers.

8.    Now I know, even an alien from outer space needs a friend!

9.    I'll never forget playing in the championship soccer match, even though we lost. I was happy just to be there with the rest of the team.

10.    My sister and I become best friends the day we built the giant sand castle together.

11.    We lost Grandpa that summer, and my life will never be the same. How could one man have taught us all so much?

# Story Glove in Action

Name_____Date_____

You can see the **Story Glove** in action by reading an exciting fiction book. As the plot unfolds, think about the different "fingers" of the Story Glove and how they fit into the story. Answer and discuss the following questions with your class:

**grabber**

1. What happens in the very beginning of the story to **"grab"** your attention?

**problem/challenge**

2. What is the **main problem** or **challenge** of the story? (remember that there might be many little problems)

3. How does the problem or challenge affect the main character?

**action of the story**

4. What action does the main character take?

5. During the story, what complications does the main character face?

**solution**

6. What is the **solution** to the problem or challenge?

7. How does the main character help **solve** the problem or challenge?

**takeaway**

8. What is the **takeaway** at the end of the story?

# Making a Folded Book

Writing fictional narratives is only half the fun. With this paper book fold you can write and publish your own books, stories, and comic books!

Fold an 8½" sheet of paper in half horizontally. Crease.

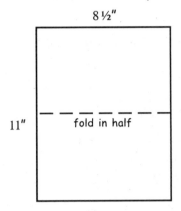

8 ½"

11"

fold in half

Fold the halves into quarters. Crease. Reverse the folds, and re-crease the opposite way so they "flip flop."

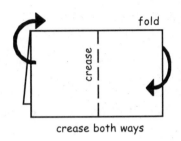

fold

crease

crease both ways

Open up to half size with the fold at the top. The quarter crease runs down the middle.

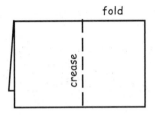

fold

crease

Fold up the long, side flap.

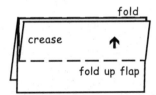

fold

crease

fold up flap

Do the same to the other side flap so both flaps have been folded up. Crease.

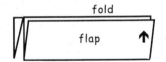

fold

flap

fold up flaps on both sides

Cut down the center line of the folded center "mountain."

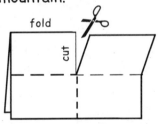

fold

cut

Pull the two cut halves down and fold the pages around to form a booklet.

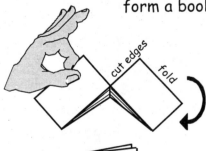

cut edges

fold

crease

You now have an eight-page book! Glue several together back to back for a longer book.

Dinosaurs

by Joey Barnard

My Dog Cocoa

by Thelma Parker

# Staying in First or Third Person

Name_____Date_____

Some stories are written in the first person. **First person means the narrator of the story is the main character, telling his own story. You will know a story is written in the first person if it uses words like *I, me,* or *my.*** Here is an example of first-person writing:

A strange, hideous noise woke **me** from a deep sleep. **I** sat straight up in bed, shaking all over from head to toe. "What is that?" **I** wondered. **My** heart was beating so hard **I** thought it might jump out of **my** chest. All of a sudden, something pounced on **me**. Something hairy. **I** screamed at the top of **my** lungs.

Other stories are written in third person. **Third person means the narrator of the story is watching the main character and all the action.** He is telling the reader the main character's story, not his own. **You will know a story is written in the third person if it uses words like *he, she, his, her, the boy, the girl,* or *a character's name.*** Here is an example of the same passage written in third person:

A strange, hideous noise woke **Cameron** from a deep sleep. **The boy** sat straight up in bed, shaking all over from head to toe. "What is that?" **he** wondered. **His** heart was beating so hard **Cameron** thought it might jump out of **his** chest. All of a sudden, something pounced on **him**. Something hairy. **He** screamed at the top of **his** lungs.

Young authors sometimes get first-person and third-person writing mixed together, and this gets confusing for the reader. When you write, stay in either first person or third person. Don't mix the two.

Read the following passage. It's a mess! Use your pencil to circle each time the author switches from first person to third person, or vice-versa.

Bailey went out to the farrowing barn to check the new baby pigs. She banged the barn door and shuffled her muck boots along the path between crates. I didn't want to be out in the barn because my favorite TV program was coming on soon. I made sure the baby pigs were underneath the heat lamp where they would stay warm. Then Bailey filled the mother sow's water and food troughs and went back to the house. I was glad my chores didn't take too long so I could watch my program.

# Practicing First and Third Person

Name_____Date_____

Write a practice paragraph about a time when something funny happened to you. Stay in the first person. This means you will use the pronouns *I, my, me,* and *myself.* When you're finished, highlight every word that indicates first-person writing.

Write a practice paragraph about something scary that happened to someone you know. Stay in third person. Be sure to use the pronouns *he, she, him, her,* or the person's name. Highlight every word that indicates third-person writing.

# NOTES

Personal Narratives

# Personal Narratives

Name_____Date_____

**When you write about an event or experience that has happened to you, it is called a *personal narrative*.** Personal narratives are sometimes called **narrative essays.** They combine elements of both expository writing and fictional narratives. In a personal narrative you might have to explain things or give your opinion as in expository writing. Yet, just like stories---fictional narratives---personal narratives **show the passing of time.**

Personal narratives are always written in the first person, and use words like *me, my, I, we,* or, *myself.* In writing a personal narrative, you might occasionally write a few details about someone else, but, most of the time, a personal narrative is about you. **The events in a personal narrative have a chronological order, so there is usually a beginning, a middle and an ending.**

Personal narratives are a good way to show your readers more about the real you: events that have happened in your life, how you feel about something in your past, and your personal history. However, you don't want to ramble on and on pointlessly. You should think of an important event or story to tell. Personal narratives need to answer the question, "So what?" You don't want someone to finish reading your personal narrative and have to say, "And your point would be...?"

**When you write a fictional story, you *create* a story that did not happen to you. When you write a personal narrative, you *re-create* an event or experience you have gone through personally.** Here is an example of a short personal narrative:

Going to the doctor is never an experience I look forward to, but my visit to Dr. Kellsington's office last week really takes the cake. First of all, I was only there for a physical exam so I could join the swim team at school. Even so, I was kind of creeped-out having to be around medical stuff and smell that alcohol-smell.

The nurse put me in a little room, and I spent another 15 minutes waiting for Dr. Kellsington to arrive. Before he came in, a nurse arrived and thought I was some other kid. She came at me with a huge hypodermic needle, saying, "Let's deaden the area and then Dr. K. can take that off for you." I panicked, let me tell you.

"I'm just here for a swim team physical!" I shouted, backing away from Nurse Needle. I wanted out of that place, fast. She stared at me strangely and then checked the name on my chart.

"Oh," she said. "I thought you were someone else."

It was enough to give a kid heart failure.

# Personal Narrative Organizer

Name_____Date_____

Try using this organizer to help you plan your personal narratives before you write.

### Personal Narrative Topic

_____

_____

### ? ? Setting Location ? ?

_____

_____

_____

### Time Frame

_____

_____

### Main Event

_____

_____

_____

### Sensory Details

_____

_____

_____

_____

_____

_____

### Emotional Feelings and Reactions

_____

_____

_____

_____

### Takeaway Ending

_____

_____

_____

# Personal Narrative Example

Name_____Date_____

Try using this organizer to help you plan your personal narratives before you write.

### Personal Narrative Topic

THE TIME I RODE GRANDADDY'S NEW RIDING LAWN MOWER

WITHOUT PERMISSION AND HAD A DISASTER

### Setting Location ??

ON ANNA MARIA ISLAND IN

GRANDADDY'S YARD

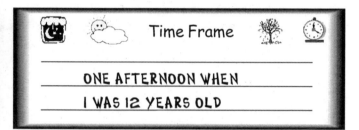

### Time Frame

ONE AFTERNOON WHEN

I WAS 12 YEARS OLD

### Main Event

GRANDADDY TELLS ME NOT TO TOUCH THE NEW MOWER. WHEN HE IS GONE

FISHING I SIT ON THE MOWER, TURN ON THE KEY, AND LOSE CONTROL.

### Sensory Details

GLEAMING LAWN MOWER

SLEEK, LUSTROUS RED

ROAR OF ENGINE

GRANDADDY YELLING

ME SCREAMING

THICK GRASS

LEATHER SEAT

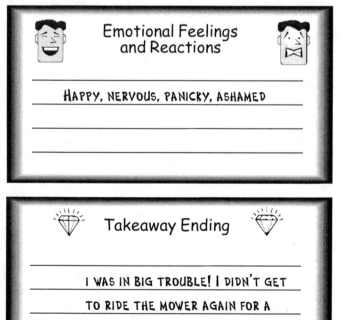

### Emotional Feelings and Reactions

HAPPY, NERVOUS, PANICKY, ASHAMED

### Takeaway Ending

I WAS IN BIG TROUBLE! I DIDN'T GET

TO RIDE THE MOWER AGAIN FOR A

LONG TIME.

Personal Narrative Example...continued

# Caught in the Act!

<sup>Grabber</sup>           <sup>Time Frame</sup>

Something happened to me the summer of my 12th year that I've never been able to live down.

<sup>Metaphor</sup>

My family refers to it as the "Riding Lawn Mower Event," but I remember it as "The Nightmare."

<sup>Setting</sup>      <sup>Setting</sup>

I was visiting my grandparents, who lived on a small coastal island on the Gulf of Mexico.

<sup>Emotional Reaction</sup>

Grandaddy's yard was his pride and joy. He had just bought a brand new riding lawn mower--his first

<sup>Sensory Detail</sup>      <sup>Sensory Detail</sup>

ever-- to cut his thick St. Augustine grass. The mower was a beauty, sleekly built and a

<sup>Sensory Detail</sup>

lustrous red. Everyone else saw it as a riding mower, but to me--in my pre-driver's-license

<sup>Metaphor</sup>    <sup>Metaphor</sup>    <sup>Metaphor</sup>

days--it was a chariot, a Corvette, a Lamborghini, begging to be taken for a spin.

<sup>Emotional Reaction</sup>

I was overjoyed when Grandaddy agreed to teach me to ride the mower after he

returned from fishing, but he warned me not to touch it until then, when he could show me

every safety precaution. However, when he left, he made the mistake of leaving the keys in

the mower's ignition. I don't need to tell you that it wasn't too long before I found myself sitting on

<sup>Sensory Detail</sup>      <sup>Sensory Detail</sup>

the mower's molded leather seat, making sound effects, pretending to drive the Daytona 500. After a

<sup>Strong Verb</sup>

while, I noticed the key and, before I could stop myself--before I could think reasonably--I cranked

the engine. V-a-r-o-o-m!

<sup>Sensory Details</sup>

My plan was to turn it on just for a moment, to feel the roar and thrust of the throttle, but

<sup>Sensory Detail</sup>

for some reason the mower was in gear and started forward with a mighty jerk. Unprepared, I lost my

<sup>Sensory Detail</sup>    <sup>Strong Verb</sup>    <sup>Sensory Detail</sup>

balance, barely hanging on. The mower surged ahead, circling crazily around the yard, bits of

<sup>Sensory Detail</sup>    <sup>Strong Verb</sup>    <sup>Sensory Detail</sup>    <sup>Simile</sup>

St. Augustine grass flying behind me. I gripped the steering wheel and yelled like a maniac. In my

<sup>Emotional Reaction</sup>      <sup>Sensory Detail</sup>

panic, I couldn't remember how to stop the mower or slow it down. I continued to circle the yard, full

<sup>Sensory Detail</sup>      <sup>Sensory Detail</sup>

speed ahead, cutting deep, irregular swaths of grass. No one was home to help me or hear my shrieks

<sup>Sensory Detail</sup>

of terror. I lost track of how many times I circled, bumping over tree roots and gopher holes.

<sup>Emotional Reaction</sup>

Finally, in desperation, I drove down the unpaved road that led to Grandaddy's fishing spot.

<sup>Sensory Detail</sup>      <sup>Sensory Detail</sup>

Billows of powdery dirt rose up behind me in a huge cloud, announcing my approaching arrival. To this

<sup>Emotional Reaction</sup>

day I can still see him running towards me, a look of disbelief on his face,

<sup>Sensory Detail</sup>

mouth open, shouting things I could not hear over the roar of the engine.

<sup>Strong Verb</sup>

Grandaddy shut off the mower and growled, "Have you lost your

ever-loving mind?"

<sup>Takeaway</sup>

I've since learned not to touch things that aren't mine!

# Personal Narrative Writing Prompts

Name_____Date_____

Personal narratives re-create something that has happened to us. Here are some prompts that might help trigger experiences, details, feelings, examples, and memories.

1   Family reunions are always interesting. Write about the last time your family got together.

2   Write a diary of your life for three days. Keep track of all the events and your feelings.

3   Think back to a time when you took a trip somewhere. Write about your favorite memories of the trip.

4   Tell about the worst school experience you've ever had.

5   Write about one hard lesson you had to learn as a child.

6   Have you ever met a hero? Tell about a time you met someone you really looked up to.

7   Write about a time when you disappointed someone you respect and how you tried to make things right.

8   Sometimes it's not a good idea to listen to our friends. Write about a time when you listened to a friend and things didn't turn out well.

9   What is something exciting that happened to you?

Personal Narrative Prompts...continued

10  All kids love to discover things. Write about a time you discovered something special.

11  Learning is part of life. Write about a time when you learned how to do something and who taught you.

12  Acts of kindness add beauty to our lives. Write about a time someone did something very kind for you.

13  Every now and then we all goof up and do something we shouldn't. Write about a time you got in trouble.

14  What is your favorite possession? Write about how you came to own this valuable possession.

15  Write about a time when you got hurt and had to have medical help.

16  What is a favorite memory you have of doing something special with your mother, father, or another person you care about?

17  What is the most interesting field trip you've been on? What made the trip memorable?

18  Write about a time you had to perform something on the stage or participate in an athletic event.

# NOTES

# Expository Writing

# Four Categories of Expository Writing

Name_____Date_____

Not everything we read or write is a story or a personal narrative. Many pieces are written to give the reader information or explanations about someone or something. This kind of writing is called **expository writing**.

There are four basic categories of expository writing:

# Information

**Characteristics:** Facts, Examples, Details, Personal Experience
**Examples:** Reports, Informative Speeches, Research, Essays, Poetry, Brochures, Introductions, Teaching, Presentations, Memoirs, Messages, Letters, Biographies, Autobiographies, Experiments, Testimonies, Itineraries

# Directions

**Characteristics:** Steps, Stages, Examples, Reasons, Transitions, Details
**Examples:** How-To Paragraphs, Recipes, Travel Directions, Instructions, Projects, Game Rules, Explanations, Coaching, Patterns, Schedules, Commands, Drills, Orders, Tutoring

# Opinions

**Characteristics:** Reasons, Examples, Personal Experience, Details, Unique Viewpoint, Comparisons, Contrasts, Preferences, Likes, Dislikes, Guesses, Theories, Beliefs
**Examples:** Personal Opinions, Reviews, Comparisons, Value Judgments, Speeches, Poetry, Greeting Cards, Letters, Complaints, Recommendations, Suggestions

# Persuasion

**Characteristics:** Reasons, Imperatives, Support of the Premise, Appeal to the Emotion of the Reader, Logic, Arguments, Convictions
**Examples:** Debates, Courtroom Scenes, Political Rallies, Discussions with Parents, Sales-Pitches, Advertising, Travel Brochures, Mediation, Peacemaking, Job Interviews, Coaching, Critiquing, Self-Defense, Invitations

# Examples of Expository Writing

Name_____Date_____

Expository writing covers a lot of ground: information, directions, opinions, and persuasion. Here are some examples of the four kinds of expository writing.

## Information          The Body's Workhorse

Out of all the parts of your body, the heart deserves the gold medal for performance. Even before you were born, your heart was beating, never to stop until the day you die. That's amazing, when you consider the only rest the heart gets is in between beats or when it slows while you are sleeping.

Imagine this: the average heart rate for a ten year old kid is eighty beats per minute. That's over 42 million beats per year. In a year's time, the heart pumps more than 500,000 gallons of blood, enough to fill 100 swiming pools. That's quite a job for a muscle no bigger than the size of your clenched fist.

If you exercise, get excited, or even frightened, the heart will increase its beats per minute to supply the body's increased need for blood. It keeps going, beat after beat after beat. Although everyone knows Arnold Schwarzenneger can pump an incredible amount of iron, not even he is a match for the human heart, the tiny workhorse of the human body.

## Directions          M-m-m-m Good!

If you're tired of the same old munchies, here's a great snack for you. Don't worry if you don't know how to cook. This is such an easy recipe that just about anyone can make these delicious cookies.

First of all, pre-heat your oven to 325 degrees. By the time you're ready to bake the cookies, the oven will be just right. Put one cup (eight ounces) of your favorite peanut butter in a big bowl. On top of the peanut butter, pour one cup of sugar. The next step is to break an egg on top of the sugar. It looks like a big, gloopy mess, but it's going to turn out great!

Now, stir these three ingredients together, and you'll notice they form a thick dough. Spray a cookie sheet with a few spritzes of no-stick cooking spray so the cookies won't stick. Using a teaspoon, form the dough into small balls. It helps if you wet your hands a little, first. Roll the balls in some sugar and place them in rows about two inches apart on the cookie sheet. Flatten the balls with the tines of a fork, forming a criss-cross pattern. Bake the cookies for 10-12 minutes, or until they are a light golden brown.

When the cookies come out of the oven, allow them to cool for five minutes on the cookie sheet. Then, scoop them up with a spatula, and transfer them to a cooling rack or a plate. Now it's time for your reward. Gobble up as many as you can before your friends and family discover you've just made the world's best peanut butter cookies! M-m-m-m.

Examples of Expository Writing...continued

## Opinion        Jean Craighead George

My favorite author, by far, is Jean Craighead George, the author of *Julie of the Wolves*, *Julie*, and *The Talking Earth*. Her books transport me to exotic settings, like the tundra of Alaska and the Florida Everglades. Her main characters are often young people who are lost in the wilderness and have to make their own way. The dire situations they get in and the dangers they face make you want to read quickly to find out what will happen next.

Jean Craighead George's books are full of ideas on how to survive out in the wilderness on your own, which is something I find fascinating. I learned how to find food among the roots of a tree, how to make a shelter from sabal palm fronds, and how to start a fire. So, not only do I like her stories, but I learn things that might help me someday.

I e-mailed Jean Craighead George to ask her a question, and she wrote me right back. She was friendly and genuinely interested in what I had to say. What makes her a good author? She has travelled all over the world and collects interesting facts to put in her books. But more than that, she's a great storyteller.

I've read everything she's written so far, and I can't wait until her next book comes out so I can read it, too. Jean Craighead George is my number-one author.

## Persuasive        Come With Me

Too many kids spend time cooped up inside all day. Do something different, for a change. Come with me canoeing down the Peace River. We'll have a fantastic time, and you can see the Florida backwoods firsthand. Since I've lived on the river all my life, I make a pretty good guide.

The Peace River is rather slow and silent, so you can take your time to explore all the things around you, such as alligators, turtles, otters, snakes, and racoons, as well as anhingas, egrets, and a million different insects. The trees that grow overhead provide a shady canopy, sheltering a variety of flowers and fruits underneath. I'll do the paddling while you enjoy the scenery and take pictures. Bring lots of film!

Looking for fossils on the Peace River is an experience never to be forgotten. You can find them just by dredging handfuls of bottom sand and mud and letting the water run through your fingers until you are left with large particles. You might find alligator teeth, Indian beads, pieces of turtle shell, vertebrae of various animals, sharks' teeth, and believe it or not, even wooly mammoths' teeth!

I've got all the supplies we need: canoe, paddles, sunscreen, insect repellent, and a full picnic basket. What are we waiting for? Join me for a relaxing, memorable time on the Peace River for a day you'll be talking about the rest of your life.

# List of Details

Name_____Date_____

Creating a list of details is a fun activity that trains you to look with a critical eye, like authors do. Many people, even adults, don't write descriptively because they don't take time to notice the details. When you think about a location or setting for a story, ask yourself some questions:

What smells would I smell? What are the colors or textures I would see? Do any particular sounds come to mind? What objects or people would I see? How would I get there? Why is this location a good choice in which to set a story?

For instance, here is a list of details about a professional baseball game:

### A BASEBALL GAME

| | | |
|---|---|---|
| crowds | peanuts | fear |
| ball players | organ music | victory |
| uniforms | scoreboard | dugout |
| grass mowed in stripes | fans | vendors |
| hot dog seller | families | the press |
| announcer | buttery popcorn | stomping |
| shouts | national anthem | cheering |
| diamond | stomping feet | jeering |
| bases | the "wave" | sweating |
| little kids | umpires | pitching |
| sunny | autographs | outfielding |
| "thwack" | disappointment | bats and balls |
| "smack" | "Strike one!" | "You're OUT!" |
| "Safe!" | "Take Me Out to the Ballgame" | home plate |

Notice there is no particular order to the list. The author just recorded thoughts as they came to her mind, jotting them down as quickly as possible. With this many sensory details, it would be easy to write a story or an expository essay about a baseball game.

Practice making lists of details from the following topics. Try to include as many sensory images as you can: **taste, smell, touch, hearing,** and **seeing.**

| | | |
|---|---|---|
| stuff in the refrigerator | a picnic in the park | in an ancient Egyptian tomb |
| things to do on a Saturday | in a mad scientist's laboratory | in the tropical rain forest |
| on a camping trip | on a bike ride through the country | in a magic show |
| at the county fair | on a mountain climbing expedition | in the chimpanzee exhibit |
| in a doctor's office | at a wild basketball game | in a clown's dressing room |
| on the African savanna | building a snowman | at a salad bar |
| in a kindergarten class | stuff in a First Aid kit | at a wrestling match |
| on a pirate ship | things in a tool chest | in a horse stable |
| at the mall food court | on an ocean voyage | in a shark tank |
| in the movie theater lobby | in a Wild West show | at the playground |
| up in a hot-air balloon | making valentines | a day at the beach |

# Writing with Details

Name_____Date_____

Just a few details in your writing make all the difference in the world. What questions do you have after you read this piece?

I love it when my friend Anisabell comes over to spend the night on Friday nights. We stay up late and do many things. We have a blast together. We fix snacks and do fun things. Sometimes we go places. I always look forward to the good times we have.

Readers want lots of details so they can picture things in their minds. Be sure you explain what you mean. Don't assume someone will know what you mean when you write these kinds of sentences:

? ? ?

? I like to <u>play</u> with my friends.

For my birthday I got a lot of <u>stuff</u>.

We go <u>many places</u>. ?

? My friend and I do <u>many things</u>. ?

I have <u>fun</u>. ?

Playing or having fun can mean a variety of things. Tell your reader the types of things you do to play or have fun and describe it so he can draw a mental picture. Here's an example:

On Saturday afternoons, my friends and I meet under the giant old oak tree near the park. We ride our bikes through the woods and look for animals. Sometimes we stop and climb a gigantic tree that has wooden slats nailed to it to form stairs. I like to sit way up top and hold on to the rough branches. Other times, my friends and I use Benjy's metal detector to hunt for buried objects. Once, we found a silver charm bracelet that belonged to Mrs. Reynolds. I don't get to see my friends much during the week because we go to different schools, but we sure have a ton of fun when we get together on the weekend.

# Supporting with Reasons and Details

Name_____Date_____

When an author begins an expository piece, he makes an important statement that contains the main idea he wants to share with the reader. That statement is called the **topic sentence**. The reader expects to hear reasons, details, and examples that will support the author's statement. Some young writers forget to give these reasons and details, just like kids do with their parents. Let's listen in on the following conversation:

Kid:    Mom, can I spend the night at David Johanson's?

Mom:  No, you've had a busy week.

Kid:    So? I want to go. Please?

Mom:  Why should I let you go?

Kid:    I want to, that's why.

Mom:  You have things to do here.

Kid:    So? I want to go. I want to go!

Mom:  No, not this time, Elmer.

Kid:    Come on, Mom. Let me go. Please? PLEASE?

What a poor way for Elmer to present his case to his mother. He keeps saying the same unconvincing things over and over. No wonder she doesn't give in. The only reason Elmer gives is that he *wants* to go to David's house to spend the night. He forgot to use persuasive reasons to support his case. Here's a more convincing argument:

Kid:    Mom, I'd like talk to you about spending the night at David Johanson's.

Mom:  Yes?

Kid:    I know I've had a busy week, but David's brother just left for college and David's feeling kind of sad. He rented videos and his mom said we could order pizza. They even have a swimming pool. I'd really like to go.

Mom:  Why should I let you go?

Kid:    I've already done my chores, except for bathing Queenie, and I'll do that tomorrow afternoon. David has practice at ten in the morning and his mom said she would drop me off then so I'll be home early.

Mom:  Well...I guess there's really no reason you couldn't go...Okay, fine.

Kid:    Great, Mom. Thanks.

Supporting your writing with reasons and details is much like Elmer's discussion with his mother. Think of convincing arguments to support your opinion or viewpoint. The more reasons and details you give, the easier it will be for your reader to agree with you.

# Detail Court

A Five-Minute Play by Melissa Forney

**Bailiff:** All rise! (Judge Trudy comes in) Hear ye, hear ye, hear ye! Detail Court is now in session, The Honorable Judge Trudy, presiding. You may be seated.

**Judge Trudy:** Bailiff, what is our first case?

**Bailiff:** The people versus the young writer.

**Judge Trudy:** We'll hear the case *against.* The prosecution may proceed.

**District Attorney:** Thank you, Your Honor. The defendant wrote an expository piece and failed to support his topic sentence with reasons and details. (audience gasps)

**Writing Teacher:** No! It can't be true! I taught those skills! I tell you, I TAUGHT THOSE SKILLS!!

**Judge Trudy:** (pounds gavel) Order in the court. No more outbursts. This isn't a circus. While I'll admit this is a very serious accusation, I'll ask the audience to control itself. I'll hear the evidence now. Proceed.

**District Attorney:** Thank you, Your Honor. I have in my hand Exhibit A, the writing in question. As you can see, the topic sentence makes the following statement: *Our school is a great place to get an education.* However, there is not one shred of evidence in this expository piece to back up that statement.

**Defense Attorney:** Objection! The student *did* support that statement with reasons and details.

**Judge Trudy:** Overruled. We haven't heard all the evidence. Continue.

**District Attorney:** My friend, Mr. Defense Attorney, suggests there *are* supporting reasons and details. Well let's see about that, shall we? Here are your so-called supporting details: *(reads from piece) We do many things to learn at school. We play and have fun. We do special things in all of our classes. Our teachers help us learn so we can have a good future.*

**Defense Attorney:** Exactly! These *are* reasons and details why the school is good.

**Judge Trudy:** I'm sorry, Counselor, but I'll have to agree with the prosecution. These pitiful, so-called reasons and details are much too general. When a young writer writes a topic sentence, it must be supported with *specific details and reasons.* Would the student please rise?

**Student:** Yes, Your Honor?

**Judge Trudy:** Weren't you in my court a few months ago on exactly the same charges?

**Student:** (ashamed) Yes, Your Honor.

**Judge Trudy:** (voice rising) And didn't I warn you that I was looking for specific details and reasons in your expository writing?

**Student:** Yes, Your Honor, but I thought *We play and have fun* was specific.

**Judge Trudy:** (angry) Don't try to mislead this court. You know better than that. Do you think I was born yesterday? What do you mean by *play?*

## Detail Court...continued

**Student:** We play science games that teach us about the solar system. Our language arts teacher lets us play a baseball game on the board that teaches us new vocabulary words. It's a blast.

**Judge Trudy:** I see. And, what do you mean by *fun*?

**Student:** That's easy. During recess we play kickball, dodgeball, tag, and shoot hoops.

**Judge Trudy:** So you *can* give specific reasons and details. Why didn't you put those in your essay? It would have made your writing much more interesting and mature.

**Student:** I...uh...I guess *play* and *fun* are...quicker...to write.

**Judge Trudy:** Just as I thought. You were being lazy. How do you expect the reader to know what you're talking about if you don't say what you mean? I warned you about this last time, didn't I?

**Student:** (tearful) Yes, Your Honor, you warned me...I just didn't listen.

**District Attorney:** You have a writing teacher. Did she or did she not teach you to support your writing?

**Student:** She did. I...just...didn't do it.

**District Attorney:** I rest my case.

**Judge Trudy:** Mr. Defense Attorney, do you have anything else to say?

**Defense Attorney:** (defeated) No, Your Honor. In light of what we've heard, the defense rests.

**Judge Trudy:** The court finds the young writer guilty as charged. (to kid) You're what we call a repeat offender and I should give you the maximum penalty.

**Student:** (desperate) Please, I promise I won't do it again. Next time I'll be very specific and give lots of supporting reasons and details.

**Judge Trudy:** You'll never mature as a writer if society keeps letting you get away with sloppy, unsupported writing.

**Student:** But I'll remember next time! I throw myself on the mercy of the court.

**Judge Trudy:** I could sentence you to two years of hard labor at the State Corrections Facility for Indolent Writers. However, I will show mercy this time. You are hereby sentenced to three months in the Boot Camp for Slothful Offenders. Bailiff, hand the prisoner over to Sergeant Strongwill.

**Bailiff:** Good luck, Kid. See you around.

**Sergeant:** Prisoner, fall out! (sings marching song) ♫ (audience echoes)
I don't know what you've been taught (I don't know what you've been taught)
♫ Lazy writers all get caught (Lazy writers all get caught)
When you're writing to impress (When you're writing to impress)
Supporting details are the best (Supporting details are the best)
Sound off (one, two ) Sound off (three, four)
Sound off-- three, four--one, two--three, four! ♫

# Writing a Basic Expository Paragraph

Name_____Date_____

Before you could work with woodworking tools to build a dog house, you would have to learn a few basics of carpentry. When it comes to expository writing, all writers should learn how to write a basic paragraph. The skills you learn will help you in all other writing. Here is an example of a basic paragraph.

## A Good Day on the Arkansas River

Sometimes I like to get away from all my friends and family and go fishing by myself. We live on the Arkansas River, and the fishing is excellent. Before I leave the house, I gather all the stuff I need: fishing pole, extra hooks, fishing line, an old bucket, bait, and something cold to drink. That's a lot of stuff for a kid to carry, so I take a small tackle box and strap the pole to my bike. Once I get to my fishing spot under a big tree, I bait my hook with a fat worm, cast it out over the water, and settle back to wait for a fish. I lie back on the soft grass, stare up at the clouds, and wait for the "big one"--a rainbow trout--to bite. Sometimes I lie there a long time, just thinking about things. When a trout hits my bait, I reel him in, take him off the line, and put him in my bucket. I know there will be fish for supper. I look forward to these lazy days when I can fish, daydream, and enjoy being by myself on the Arkansas River.

Notice the basic paragraph has a certain pattern to it. It starts out by telling the reader something important:

Sometimes I like to get away from all my friends and family and go fishing by myself.

Then the paragraph tells the reader a variety of details about getting ready and going fishing. The author finishes by summing up her experience in a single sentence:

I look forward to these lazy days....

**When writing a basic expository paragraph, tell the reader something important, give many details that answer who, what, when, where, why, or how. Finish by summing up your thoughts with a concluding sentence.**

# Writing a Basic Paragraph

Name_____Date_____

 **Step One:  Write a list of details.**

As soon as you've settled on a topic for your paragraph, write or jot down everything you can think of about it. Get your thoughts on paper. Use sensory details to help create the list of details. For instance, if you are going to write about your dog, Max, make a quick list of how you got him, the way he looks, how you feel about him, what you do together, etc. You can organize these details into a web or storyboard or leave them in a simple list.

After you've compiled the list, look it over. Narrow your list to 8-15 details you can write about in a single paragraph. Cross out the other details you decide not to use.

 **Step Two:  Create a main idea.**

Look carefully at the list of details. The combination of details should produce a main idea. Something like *I love my dog, Max, even though he's a pain in the neck*, or, *Max is a pretty good old boy*.  By analyzing your list of details, you should get a general idea of an important statement you'd like to make and support.

 **Step Three:  Write a topic sentence.**

The main idea is just a thought. To write a topic sentence, expand the main idea into an interesting sentence that let's your reader know right away what your paragraph is going to be about. For instance, if your main idea is *I love my dog*, your topic sentence could be something like *The world's greatest dog lives at my house*, or, *I'm in love with an 85-pound mutt named Max.*

 **Step Four:  Support with detail sentences.**

Here's where the list of details is really going to help you. Looking over the list,  combine three or even four details that go together into one well-written sentence. *Max leaps into bed with me on stormy nights and buries his shaggy, brown body under the covers.* Now amplify that sentence with a follow-up sentence. *There's not much room in my bed for two of us, but I feel sorry for him when he's shaking and scared.*

 **Step Five:  Sum up your thoughts with a conclusion.**

The very end of your paragraph is a good time to remind the reader of your most important statement. If the main idea is, *I love my dog, Max*, tell that to the reader one more time. Of course, it would be boring to use the same exact words you used in the topic sentence, so choose another, creative way. *Of all the dogs in the whole world, I'm glad Max, the wonder dog, is my best friend.*

 **Step Six:  Revise your writing by adding appropriate target skills.** ◎

Read your paragraph carefully to make sure you've included writing target skills such as strong verbs, sizzling vocabulary words, similes, metaphors, onomatopoeia, etc. These elements of creativity add drama, beauty, and interest.

# Organizing Multiple Paragraghs

Name_____Date_____

When you are going to write several paragraphs, start with an introduction. **An introduction is a general sentence that sets up the topic sentence.** Next, write a strong topic sentence that tells the reader the most important thing you want to say. Explain and expand that main idea.

Change paragraphs when you change locations, time, speakers, subjects, or when you want to highlight a specific point of the main topic. Add transitional phrases and detail sentences. Remember, each new paragraph needs its own topic sentence, detail sentences, and conclusion. End your piece with a powerful conclusion by restating your main idea in a fresh way.

This piece on Italy, which is an information piece written in first person, demonstrates how to organize multiple paragraphs.

*Italy*

↓ Introduction
Would you believe you can actually fall in love with a country? Last summer, I
↓ topic sentence
took a two-week trip to beautiful, sunny Italy. My mother had always wanted to see

"the old country," and invited me to go with her. During the weeks before we left on

our trip, I tried to imagine the incredible sights we would soon see.
↓ topic sentence
Our fascinating journey took us all over the country of Italy, starting in Rome.

We visited the Coliseum, where the ancient Romans staged gladiator fights, and saw

the modern-day Gypsies, who sell things outside the gates. At Vatican City, my mother

and I looked at priceless art treasures, like the Pietà and Michelangelo's statue of

David. I couldn't stop staring at the ceiling in the Sistine Chapel. Everywhere my

eyes looked were more portraits and elaborate backgrounds. Rome was so full of
↓ conclusion
places to go and things to buy we could have stayed there for days and days.
↓ transitional phrase    ↓ topic sentence
The next part of our journey took us north to Genoa, where Columbus set sail

to the new world, and Milan, the fashion capitol of Italy. The Italian people enjoy

beautiful clothes and wearing them with a great deal of style. My mother and I drank

capuccino and sat in the piazza for hours, just to watch and admire. We enjoyed
↓ conclusion
buying leather purses and stationery in Florence. Northern Italy was awesome.

Italy...continued

↓ topic sentence
One of my favorite experiences was my visit to the Blue Grotto.

After taking a ship to Capri, we changed to a smaller boat and set off

for the Blue Grotto, a hidden cave in a natural rock formation. Our boat

anchored in deep water, and we paid an Italian fisherman to take us into

the grotto in a small row boat. I trembled from head to toe because the waves were

crashing right at the opening of the cave. My mother and I had to lie down in the

bottom of the row boat while the fisherman pulled on two chains and swept us into the

dark, hidden cave. It was exciting and dangerous at the same time. The water below us

was lit up like a glowing, peacock-blue jewel. The walls of the cave rippled and shim-
↓ conclusion
mered. It was almost too beautiful to describe in words.
↓ transitional phrase          ↓ topic sentence
After this incredible experience, we headed to Venice, in northeast Italy. The

entire city was built hundreds of years ago on wooden pilings over the water. Instead

of normal, paved streets, Venice has water canals. The Italians pole long, ornate, flat

boats called gondolas through the canals to get where they want to go. Our gondolier

sang Italian songs as we glided through the city of Venice. While we were in Venice,

we visited the glass blowers, who use the same method of blowing glass that was used
↓ conclusion
there a thousand years before. I never wanted to leave the unique city of Venice.
↓ transitional phrase                              ↓ topic sentence
As I look back over my trip to Italy, I realize it was the trip of a lifetime.

There are more wonderful sights and memories than I have time to tell: visiting the

Tower of Pisa, watching pizza being made in Naples, going to the Duomo, and eating

delicious gelati, Italian ice cream. I've never seen such a beautiful, interesting country

as Italy. When I threw my three coins in Rome'sTrevi Fountain, my Italian friends
↓ conclusion
promised me I would one day return. I hope they are right, because enchanting Italy

won my heart.

# Five-Paragraph Essay

Name_____Date_____

One classic, formal piece of expository writing is a five-paragraph essay. Its five paragraphs follow a pattern that is commonly used in educational settings. Understandably, this piece is called a **five-paragraph essay**. You will more than likely be asked to write many five-paragraph essays throughout your education. A five-paragraph essay is a convenient way to organize your thoughts into a format the reader can easily follow.

The standard pattern of the five-paragraph essay is as follows:

## Paragraph 1

| | |
|---|---|
| Introduction | Grabs the reader/Sets up the topic sentence |
| Topic Sentence | The most important statment overall |
| Three Main Thoughts | Three reasons the topic sentence is true |
| Conclusion | Sums up this paragraph's main thought |

## Paragraph 2

| | |
|---|---|
| Topic Sentence | Main thought #1 |
| Detail Sentences | Support with reasons, examples, and details |
| Concluding sentence | Sums up this paragraph's main thought |

## Paragraph 3

| | |
|---|---|
| Topic Sentence | Main thought #2 |
| Detail Sentences | Support with reasons, examples, and details |
| Concluding sentence | Sums up this paragraph's main thought |

## Paragraph 4

| | |
|---|---|
| Topic Sentence | Main thought #3 |
| Detail Sentences | Support with reasons, examples, and details |
| Concluding sentence | Sums up this paragraph's main thought |

## Paragraph 5

| | |
|---|---|
| Topic Sentence | Restates the most important statement |
| Restate | Repeat the three main thoughts |
| Conclusion | Leave the reader with a final summary thought |

# Five-Paragraph Essay Example

Name_____Date_____

## Resources From the Sea

grabber/introduction

When you look at a globe, you can't help but notice

that a good portion of the Earth is covered by water.

most important statement

<u>The oceans of the world are splendid resources that enrich</u>

<u>our lives in more ways than we could possibly count.</u> The

main thought #1            metaphor

sea provides us with a smorgasbord of delicious things to eat. The oceans are

metaphor                main thought #2

also much-used highways for transportation and commerce. Millions of people

main thought #3

enjoy water sports and the natural beauty the seaside offers. Earth's oceans

conclusion        simile

and seas are like survival resources for all people.

transitional phrase                        main thought #1

<u>First of all, the bounty of the sea provides food for people all over the</u>

strong verb       detail

<u>world.</u> Fishermen in Alaska earn their living by harvesting king crabs and

detail

salmon. Giant tuna are caught in South American waters and canned. Fresh

detail

Maine lobsters are not only delicious, but provide a living for thousands of

detail

fishermen and their families. A few cultures of people still hunt whales as a

detail  detail        detail         detail     detail        detail

source of food, oil, and medicine. Octopus, squid, and clams are popular dishes

detail     detail

in the Mediterranean regions. Russian fish eggs, called caviar, are considered

detail

to be a delicacy. Around the world people eat a variety of fish, which are not

detail                              detail        detail

only delicious, but provide an important source of protein and iodine. The

metaphor                conclusion

sea's bounty is plentiful, useful, and nutritious.

transitional phrase

Here is another thought to consider. Most of us are used to traveling

main thought #2

by car and airplane, but did you know the <u>busiest highway on Earth is the</u>

detail

<u>ocean?</u> In some cultures, boats are the primary method of getting from one

detail                        strong verb

place to another. Millions of tons of goods are transported around the world

detail

by giant ships which navigate major shipping lanes. People who live on remote

## Five Paragraph Essay Example...continued

detail
islands are dependent on boats for their food, living supplies, and news of
detail                                                    detail
the outside world. The sight of a distant ship on the horizon brings them joy
detail                              amplified detail
and anticipation. Medical ships, called floating hospitals, drop anchor near
detail                        detail      detail
poor countries and provide modern medicine and surgery for people who
detail                    detail    detail
don't have local doctors and nurses to care for them. In times of war, oceans
detail
allow navies to defend their coastlines or to reach distant ports quickly.
conclusion
Earth's many oceans provide a steady flow of transportation for

commerce, supplies, medical help, and military defense.
transitional phrase
Let's move on to the more enjoyable aspects of the sea. The ocean is
main thought #3        metaphor                                detail
nature's original playground. Families can picnic, swim, jet ski, collect shells,
detail  detail                              detail                    detail
and build sand castles at the water's ebbing edge. Small children play
detail              detail        detail                detail
in the shallow water and float on blow-up rafts and toys. Older kids dive
detail          detail              detail            detail
for sand dollars and starfish or hunt for special shells and driftwood. Even
detail
if you don't want to go swimming, you can sit in the shade of a large umbrella
detail              detail    detail              detail
and enjoy watching surfers, water skiers, snorkelers, and parasailers. Scuba
detail      detail              detail              detail
divers search the depths for sunken treasures and rare species of sea crea-
detail
tures. The ocean has so many things to offer that many people choose to live
detail              conclusion
right at its shore. Calm or stormy, the surf provides beauty,

enjoyment, and entertainment.
restates most important statement              main thought #1
The entire world relies on the sea. A delicious meal is just at the end

of our fishing poles. We can follow in the steps of Marco Polo and Columbus
main thought #2
by sailing around the world to any port that will welcome us. Stepping into
main thought #3
the water's edge can provide a variety of enjoyable activities and

sports. There are many wonders on this incredible Earth, but few
final summary thought
offer such rich resources as the magnificent oceans around us.

# Expository Grabbers

Name_____Date_____

Who says grabbers are only for narratives? Some of the best expository pieces start out with sentences that capture the reader's attention. Here are some examples:

1  ## Rhetorical Question
Why do adults insist that kids have to go to bed so early on school nights?

2  ## Dialogue
"Touchdown! The Dallas Cowboys win the Super Bowl again!"

3  ## Mystery Statement
Deep down in the ocean lurks a dangerous killing machine.

4  ## Shocking Statement
Stone Cold Steve Austin, WWF superstar, is going to be our substitute teacher tomorrow!

5  ## Humorous Statement
Don't ask me why, but my little sister can get into more trouble than a bunch of monkeys on the loose.

6  ## Onomatopoeia
Crash! Ka-blam! Car wrecks can happen at any speed, so it's important to wear your seatbelt at all times.

7  ## Personal Opinion
In my opinion, mountain biking is more fun than going to the mall or playing video games.

8  ## Strong Persuasive Statement
Every kid who cares about the future of the Camera Club should vote for Jackson Tyler as our new club president.

# Expository Topic Sentences

Name_____Date_____

Every paragraph needs one main point. **The topic sentence expresses the main point and lets the reader know what the paragraph is going to be about.** However, the topic sentence does not have specific details in it.

topic sentence
<u>Every night before I go to bed I have to take a shower</u>. I just can't sleep without it. You see, all day long at school I get cruddy, especially at lunch and P.E. and art. After school, I play basketball with my friends and get sweaty and hot, so naturally, I'm stinky. At night, when I want to relax and go to sleep, I like to feel clean. Believe me, I need that shower!

The paragraph would sound silly without the topic sentence. The reader would have no idea what the writer was talking about.

Before you write a topic sentence, quickly jot down a list of details about your topic. After looking at the list carefully, think of the main thing you want to say about your topic. This will be your main point. Now include that main point in your topic sentence. Don't include details in your topic sentence. They'll come later in the detail sentences. For example, here's a list of details about cleaning your house:

vacuum the floors          scrub the bathtub
dust the shelves           change the sheets
water the plants           sweep the kitchen
do the dishes              clean the bathrooms

From those eight items, you could generate many different topic sentences. What is the *main point* you want to make? Here are a few examples of the many topic sentences you could write:

✓   Cleaning our house takes up a whole Saturday morning!

✓   I would rather walk on broken glass than have to clean house.

✓   When our whole family pitches in, cleaning the house isn't so bad.

✓   We can go to the game, but first I have to help clean the house.

# Practicing Expository Topic Sentences

Name_____Date_____

Look at the following topics. For each one, make a list of details. After carefully looking at the list, think of the main idea that could be said about that subject. Write a topic sentence expressing the main idea. Do not include specific details in your topic sentences.

1. Knights and castles during Medieval times
2. Christopher Columbus' journey to the new world
3. The great pyramids of Egypt
4. The election of the President of the United States
5. Homeless kids who live on the streets
6. Flying on an airplane for the first time
7. Getting your teeth cleaned at the dentist's office
8. Having to move and change schools during the school year
9. Finding interesting stuff on the Internet
10. Spending an afternoon at the mall
11. Learning to cook for yourself
12. The amount of money movie stars are paid
13. Owning your own baby hippopotamus
14. What happens when a subsitute teacher takes over for a day
15. Learning to speak another language
16. Looking through the family scrapbook/photo album
17. Skills Eskimos have that most people don't have
18. Cleaning up after your pet
19. What happens when your friends come over
20. Getting your own bank account
21. Building a fort or tree house

# Introductions

Name_____Date_____

In most well-written expository pieces, an introductory sentence, which is called an **introduction**, comes before the topic sentence.

There is a big difference between an introduction and a topic sentence. You might know that a topic sentence expresses the main idea. It is very specific. **The introduction comes before the topic sentence and is broader, or more general.**

Here's an example of the difference between *general* and *specific*:

General = Overall, a whole category, broad = AUTOMOBILES

Specific = A particular one = CHRYSLER  PT CRUISER

An easy way to learn to write an introduction is to write your topic sentence first. Then think about the main idea and how you can introduce that idea to your reader in a  more general way.

Here's an example:

introduction - general          topic sentence - specific
It's important to be well-informed. I read the newspaper

every day so I'll know what's going on in the world.

An introduction sets up the topic sentence:

introduction - general
There are certain things every kid needs to experience at least once.
topic sentence - specific
Making your own kite and flying it with your friends is an

incredible way to spend a windy afternoon.

The introduction can also be a sentence that lets the reader know something very important is about to be said:

introduction - general
Have I got some news that will rock your world! We're getting a brand new
topic sentence - specific
baseball coach, a man by the name of Dan Gil.

# Conclusions

Name_____ Date _____

Good expository writing is full of **information**, **descriptions**, **reasons**, and **supporting details**. Some writers, though, simply stop when they can't think of anything else to say. Others write boring endings that put the reader to sleep. A good writer adds a summary sentence that reminds the reader of the most important message in the piece.

For example:

So, the next time you see a great white shark, remember that behind the ferocious teeth and cold, staring eyes is an amazing creature to be spared from senseless slaughter.

Another example:

For the rest of my life I'll always remember Miss Beth Severson, my fourth-grade teacher, and how she made our year together so unforgettable.

There are a variety of ways to begin well-written conclusions. You can add your own important message to the end of these beginnings or sum up your thoughts for the reader with an original sentence of your own.

I hope I've convinced you about the importance of....
Now you can see why....
My life will never be the same because....
I hope next time you'll stop to remember....
Let's work together to make sure....
The world would be a different place if we all....
I learned the valuable lesson that....
From now on, I'll....
I hope you can agree with me that....
One thing I know for certain is....
The truth is....
We'd all be better off if....
I wish every kid could....
So you see, it's a good idea to....
The main thing is....
I'd like to sum up my thoughts by saying....

# Restating Information

Name_____Date_____

**Restating means to say the same thing in different words.** Authors often have to restate a point to keep it fresh in the reader's mind. This is especially true when writing a conclusion. You don't want to repeat something in the exact same way you said it before. Instead, say the same thing another way.

Consider this topic sentence:

Cycling is a great way to stay in shape and have fun, too.

You might later restate that same information as:

Give cycling a chance and I think you'll like it as much as I do.

Another topic sentence might be:

Raising earthworms to sell for bait is an interesting and profitable hobby.

You could restate that thought as follows:

I never thought I'd enjoy raising earthworms, but I think the worms and I are going to be friends for a long, long time.

You might tell your audience:

My sister Ellen and I can't wait for winter to come so we can build a snowman.

If you wish to restate that thought later, be sure to use different words and a different sentence structure to add interest:

Stop by this winter so you can see the world's most beautiful snowman!

One convenient thing about the English language is we have many different ways to say the same thing. Restating is a good skill to know because it comes in so handy in your writing. Reminding your readers of your main point is the perfect way to end your piece.

# Practicing Restating Information

Name_____Date_____

Read the following sentences. Restate the same thoughts a different way.

1. If you've never watched bungee jumping you've missed something spectacular.

2. Pirates used to roam the seven seas, terrorizing sailors and passengers of other ships.

3. After school, kids should eat healthy snacks instead of junk food.

4. *Romeo and Juliet* is the saddest play I've ever seen.

5. Having a garage sale is a lot of hard work but a great way to make some money.

6. Everyone should know how to read a map.

7. There is no excitement to equal a close basketball game.

8. Some people like clowns, but I think they're scary.

9. A scarecrow is a good way to keep birds from eating your garden.

# Dialogue in Expository Writing

Name_____Date_____

Using dialogue in a story is common, but what about in an expository paragraph or essay? It's a well-kept writers' secret that dialogue can be used in expository writing, too. It can add an element of realism to a piece or set an interesting mood. One or two lines of well-written dialogue can be a great enhancement to expository writing pieces.

Take the subject of sharks, for instance. Many kids start an expository piece with a boring sentence like:

Sharks are interesting creatures.

Ho-hum. That sentence isn't going to grab your reader, is it? Try adding a line of exciting dialogue at the beginning of your piece.

"Shark! Get out of the water!" These words strike fear in the heart of anyone swimming in the ocean's edge. However, when we're brave enough to look beyond our fears, we might find the shark is really an intriguing creature.

Another method is to weave dialogue into the detail sentences as an example of what someone has said:

The Crocodile Hunter is one of my favorite guys on television. In my opinion, he has the most incredible job on Earth. When I hear him say, "Danger, danger, danger," in that Aussie accent, I can't help but laugh. It's obvious that he LOVES danger. I also think it's a riot that he says, "You little beauty!" while he's holding a hideous reptile close to his face.

Still another way to use dialogue in expository writing is to tell the reader your own opinion in a very personal, realistic way:

For weeks I've watched the television show, *Survivor*, to see what it would be like to spend 39 days in a remote location with 15 strangers. It's amazing to me to see that the survivors will eat anything: live grubs, eels, stingrays, or even rats. If I were in that situation I would be tempted to say, "Keep your million dollars. I'm NOT eating worms, now, or ever!"

# Jazzing Up Your Expository Writing

Name_____Date_____

Just because expository writing is often used to educate or inform doesn't mean it has to be dull and boring. As a matter of fact, the very best expository writing has been "jazzed up" with writing target skills that make it enjoyable for the reader.

Many young authors strive to write creatively when they're writing fictional narratives, adding in descriptions galore. However, these same creative techniques can be used to enhance your expository writing. Consider these dull expository sentences:

The manatee is an interesting water mammal. They are on the endangered species list because so many have been wounded by speeding boats. Many are killed each year. Someday there might not be any more manatees for people to see.

There's nothing *wrong* with these sentences except they are so *ordinary*. The sentences contain good information, but they sound like a thousand other reports. The facts are not presented in an interesting, creative way. **Jazz up your expository writing!** This time the author added dialogue and a few sentences in first person to create interest.

"This huge water mammal is a manatee," I'd like to be able to say to my grandchildren someday in the future. Unfortunately, I might not have the chance, since manatees might be extinct by then. Each year, speeding boat propellers gouge, injure, and kill hundreds of manatees, which are now on the endangered species list.

Read the sentences below. They sound lifeless and ordinary. Rewrite the sentences, jazzing them up with creativity, strong verbs, specific examples, descriptive writing, or imaginative dialogue.

One of my least favorite things to do is eat in the cafeteria. It's very noisy and people make a mess. I bring my own lunch every day.

Jazz it up, Mama!

_____
_____
_____
_____
_____

# Expository Writing Prompts

Name_____Date_____

Writing is just like painting a picture, or playing a sport. The more you practice, the better you get. Practice your new skills with these expository prompts.

 Let's imagine that all kids had to serve our country for one year in a special youth corps that would train them in loyalty, honor, discipline and patriotism. In your opinion, would this be a good thing or a not-so-good thing? Why?

What if traveling through time was really possible? Every adventurer dreams of the possibility of a machine that could transport living beings back to a certain period of history. If you had the opportunity to travel back in time, where and when would you go? Why would you make this choice, and what would you be most interested in seeing?

The journey to the New World with Christopher Colombus must have been hard and dangerous but challenging and exciting. Imagine being among the first explorers to see such sights! If you had been invited to join Colombus on his journey, explain why you would you have said yes, and ignored the risks, or said no, and stayed safely at home.

 Some educators think that giving kids a grade on a report card is necessary. Others think that learning in school should be a joyous experience and kids should not have to worry about grades. What is your opinion?

Expository Prompts...continued

**5** In our society, we wait until kids are grown and educated to train them for important careers. But what if things were different? If you could be trained right now at your age to start an "adult" job or career, which one would you choose, and why?

**6** Going out to eat at a restaurant is something most people look forward to. If you were going to take a special friend to your favorite place to eat, which restaurant would you choose and why? Be sure to include reasons and details that support your personal opinion.

**7** Teachers help us learn many things. Think of a teacher who has been special to you. She could be a classroom teacher, a piano teacher, a coach, or some other person who has taken the time to teach you something. Imagine you are describing this teacher to someone who has never met her before. Give examples, reasons and details to explain why this teacher is special to you.

**8** We live in a modern world of computers, machines, and appliances. Inventors have tried to make our lives easier by making things faster and more convenient. Think about the people who lived 100 years ago. They had few modern luxuries but knew how to work hard. Children knew how to plant, harvest, and make their own toys. They walked to school and played outdoors. Are we better off today, or have we grown lazy?

# NOTES

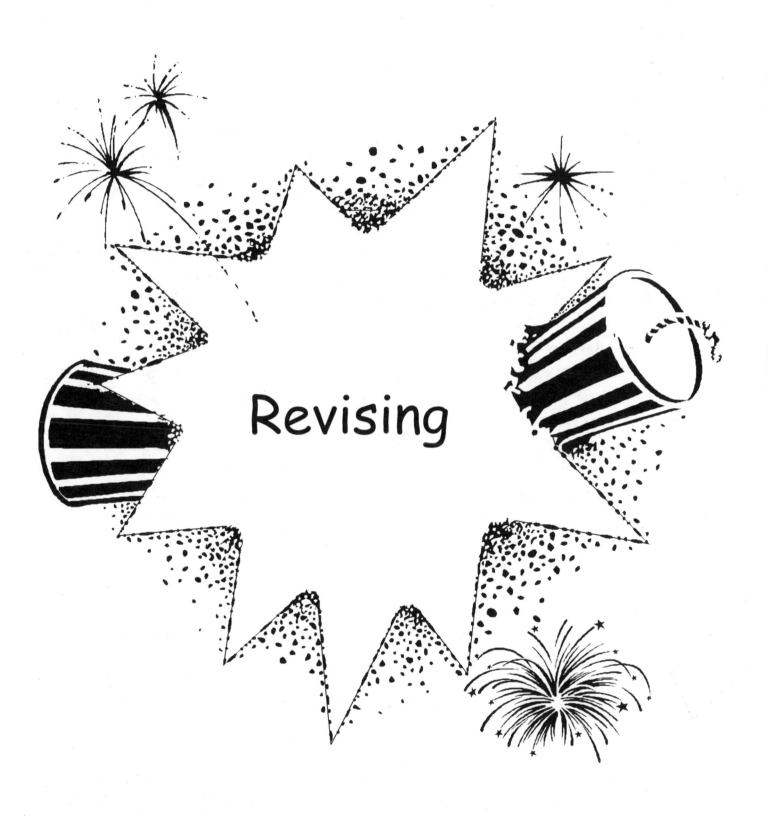

Revising

# Revising

Name_____Date_____

The number one mistake most young writers make is to write a rough draft, correct the spelling and punctuation, and think they're done. They've missed the most important step of all, **revising.**

When you write your first rough draft, you're just getting your thoughts down on paper. Your rough draft might be pretty good, but the best writing of all comes with revision. When kids read great books and stories by their favorite authors, they seldom stop to think that authors revise over and over and over---sometimes more than 50 times---so they can make sure their manuscripts are the best they can possibly be. The result of their revision is writing so detailed, so smooth, so fascinating, that we want to read all the way to the very end.

**Revision means improving your writing in big ways: adding more information, more supporting details, answering unanswered questions, or replacing ordinary, boring words with sizzling vocabulary.** Revision is not correcting spelling, neatness, or adding punctuation. Those things are taken care of in the editing process. **Editing comes after you have revised several times.**

Try this. After you've written your rough draft, read and reread it several times. Look for areas that need explanation or improvement. Don't be afraid to mark, cross out, add words to the margins, etc.

The following is an example of revision. After writing a rough draft of a story about her grandmother's childhood, the author read through it carefully. Realizing she could improve the language, she changed a few ordinary words to better ones. She also added information that would help readers form clear, mental pictures of an old-fashioned laundry day.

*enormous*

The ~~huge,~~ black wash pot had already been scrubbed with river sand the day

*fresh* *from the cistern* *and banked*
*the*
before and filled with rain water. Early this morning Mama had built a fire under the tub *coals*

Rebecca knew what Mama would want her to do without being asked. Using a sharp knife,

*shaved*
she carefully ~~cut up~~ an entire cake of lye soap into the boiling, bubbling water. *A hot,*

*steamy, soap-smell filled the yard.*

# Young Author's Revising Questions

Name_____Date_____

Answering these revision questions will help you improve your rough drafts.

☐ 1. Does the beginning grab or hook the reader's attention?

☐ 2. Are there any unanswered questions? Did I answer WHO, WHAT, WHEN, WHERE, WHY, AND HOW?

☐ 3. Can I substitute a more interesting word for a boring one?

☐ 4. Can I add more information to amplify a thought or idea?

☐ 5. Is there a statement that needs more explanation with reasons, details, or examples?

☐ 6. Do my readers need more description to be able to picture what I'm writing about?

☐ 7. Do most of my sentences start with different beginnings?

☐ 8. Is there a fresher, more interesting way to say something?

☐ 9. Did I use similes, metaphors, strong verbs, specific emotion words, sensory words, onomatopoeia, or dialogue to make my writing colorful and enjoyable for my readers?

☐ 10. Does every sentence focus on the topic?

☐ 11. Did I use transitional phrases and words between thoughts and ideas?

☐ 12. Does the ending bring this piece to a smooth finish?

# Who, What, When, Where, Why & How

Name_____Date_____

Leaving out important information in your writing can be troublesome. After they write, authors and journalists typically ask themselves, *Did I answer who? what? when? where? why? and how?* Those six little questions can save the day. When you finish a rough draft, check to see that you have answered these all-important questions. If one is missing, it's a relatively simple task to add the information you need so your writing will be complete.

Ask your teacher to laminate the sheet below. Then, cut the cards apart. Punch a hole in the top left-hand corner of each card. Hook the cards together with a metal ring. Use these cards as reminders when you get to the revision stage.

✂ _ _ _ cut out cards _ _ _ _

# Staying Focused

Name_____Date_____

What do cameras, telescopes, and writing have in common? They all have to stay focused. No one wants to take blurry pictures or look at fuzzy, hazy stars. **The word focus also means that every sentence stays on topic.** Things can get a little confusing when writing wanders around and doesn't stay on topic. The reader has no idea what the writer's real subject is. All of us tend to "chase rabbits"---get off the subject---every once in a while. All writers have to watch out for that mistake. When you finish writing a rough draft, it is important to read and reread your manuscript carefully, making sure every sentence, every paragraph, is on topic. Ask yourself, "Did I stay focused on the topic?"or, "Did I wander off the subject?" Cross out or replace sentences that wander off topic.

Read the paragraphs below. Cross out the three sentences that do not focus on the topic: having a parrot as a pet.

## "Polly Want a Cracker?"

Parrots make wonderful, funny, unusual pets. These loving birds can become very tame if you raise them from babies and treat them gently. Some breeds of dogs are like that, too.

In order to keep your parrot happy, you must provide a large birdcage in a location where he can have an outside view and also feel part of your family. Parrots love company. They chatter, sing, whistle and call in very loud voices. They love to imitate people's voices and other sounds they hear on a regular basis. Parrots require fruits, seeds, water, and vegetables every day. I hate vegetables. I'm glad I'm not a parrot.

Many parrots live more than 50 years! If you want a pet that's going to be around for a long time, and you're willing to take good care of him, you might consider a parrot.

It's pretty easy to pick out the sentences that stray off topic when you read someone else's writing, but what about in your own writing? Read and reread your rough drafts carefully to find areas of writing that do not focus on the topic.

# Stretching Your Sentences

Name_____Date_____

# 4-Page Sentence S-t-r-e-t-c-h-e-r-s

Most of the sentences we say aloud in ordinary conversation are long, detailed, and interesting. Something mysterious happens when we start to write, though. Our sentences come out short and boring. It's a good practice to look carefully at those little sentences and ask ourselves what other information we can add. These sentence stretchers will help you get in the habit of doing just that.

Start with two 8½" x 11" sheets of paper.

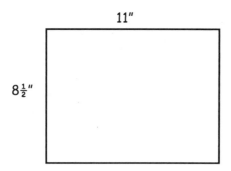

Place one sheet of paper over the other sheet, overlapping them approximately 1½".

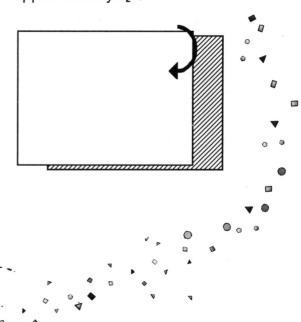

Fold the top sheet back over itself, leaving another inch-and-a-half extension.

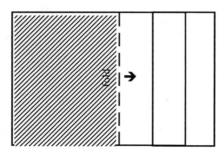

Fold the remaining bottom sheet back over itself, leaving another inch-and-a-half extension.

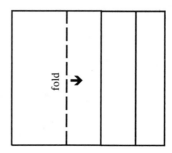

## Stretching Your Sentences...continued

Put a little glue in the top fold crease and press together so the sheets form a booklet.

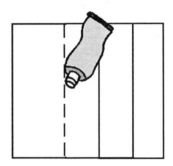

Using scissors or a paper cutter, cut the sheets into long, 4-page strips about one inch across.

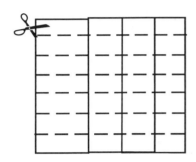

Write a simple sentence on the first page. Add details such as who, what, when, where, why, or how to each of the following pages.

Who?

1 | I went shopping.

Where?

2 | I went shopping at the mall.

What?

3 | I went shopping at the mall for a new bathing suit.

When?

4 | Last week, I went shopping at the mall for a new bathing suit.

When they're closed, your sentence stretcher will look like a skinny flip-book. What a difference between the first sentence and the last! To make it really challenging, start a sentence stretcher and pass it around a circle of other writers. Let the next three kids add new information to the previous sentence.

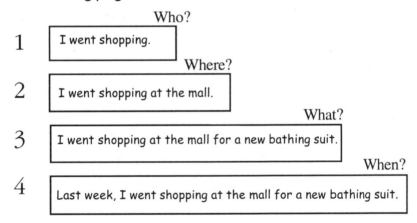

# Sizzling Vocabulary

Name_____Date_____

Why use ordinary words when we can use words that s-i-z-z-l-e? An outstanding vocabulary is one of the marks of a great writer. Lackluster words create boring material. The first passage below sounds generic and ordinary:

When Nadja's back was turned, the bull snorted and came after her. She turned and became afraid when she saw how big he was. He ran very fast.

Add a few sizzling words and the passage becomes charged with excitement.

When Nadja's back was turned, the raging bull snorted and began to charge. Turning, she flinched in terror at his monstrous size. Gargantuan! He tore across the pasture like lightning on the loose.

When they're writing rough drafts, writers often use the first word that comes into their heads. However, when revising, they look at each word. Think about the impact each word has. This is when you can choose better words or sizzling vocabulary words. Select words that convey your meaning and mood to the reader.

The dictionary and thesaurus are great places to gather words. Keep a list of sizzling vocabulary words that add splash and pizzazz to your writing. Here are a few lists to start with. Keep adding to these and other lists in your writer's notebook.

A monster in your story doesn't have to be *ugly*. He could be....

| | | | | |
|---|---|---|---|---|
| bizarre | grotesque | loathsome | revolting | undesirable |
| disgusting | hideous | monstrous | horrific | unsightly |
| dog-faced | homely | repulsive | unattractive | wretched |

On the other hand, a princess doesn't have to be just *pretty*. She could be....

| | | | | |
|---|---|---|---|---|
| adorable | chic | divine | foxy | lovely |
| appealing | comely | elegant | glamorous | magnificent |
| attractive | cute | exotic | good-looking | muy bonita |
| beautiful | dazzling | exquisite | gorgeous | striking |
| charming | desirable | fetching | handsome | stunning |

## Sizzling Vocabulary...continued

A subject you are writing about doesn't have to be just *interesting*. It could be....

| | | | | |
|---|---|---|---|---|
| absorbing | captivating | extraordinary | intriguing | remarkable |
| appealing | enthralling | fascinating | mesmerizing | spellbinding |

Something *small* could be described in many ways, such as....

| | | | | |
|---|---|---|---|---|
| bantam | Lilliputian | miniscule | petite | tiny |
| diminutive | microscopic | minute | puny | undersized |
| dwarfed | midget | paltry | small | wee |
| itsy-bitsy | miniature | pee-wee | teeny-weeny | weensy |

If one of your characters thinks something is *good*, it could be called....

| | | | | |
|---|---|---|---|---|
| awesome | excellent | fine | marvelous | super |
| delightful | exceptional | first-rate | outstanding | terrific |
| enjoyable | fantastic | great | pleasant | wonderful |

Does someone *rub you the wrong way?* He could be....

| | | | | |
|---|---|---|---|---|
| aggravating | exasperating | infuriating | loathsome | provoking |
| annoying | frustrating | irksome | maddening | trying |
| bothersome | grating | irritating | pestering | wearisome |

Words can't express how *big* something is...That is, until you try one of these....

| | | | | |
|---|---|---|---|---|
| behemoth | gargantuan | huge | leviathan | super-size |
| colossal | giant | humongous | mammoth | titanic |
| elephantine | gigantic | immense | massive | tremendous |
| enormous | Herculean | jumbo | monstrous | vast |
| epic | hippopotamic | large | stupendous | whopping |

You try not to *laugh* at something funny, but you can't help but burst out with a....

| | | | | |
|---|---|---|---|---|
| belly-laugh | chuckle | ha-ha-ha | peel of laughter | snort |
| cackle | giggle | hee-haw | roar | tee-hee |
| chortle | guffaw | hoot | snicker | whoop |

# Writing Complete Sentences

Name_____Date_____

Almost all writing is made up of sentences. Young writers must be able to construct complete sentences so readers are not confused or left with unfinished ideas. You've seen incomplete sentences before:

My fluffy, white cat Susie.   What about her?
When Dad comes home tonight.   What will happen then?
Running and playing all over the place.    Who is doing this?

These incomplete sentences raise questions. They are dead give-aways that the author didn't check his work and revise.

**Every sentence has two important parts: the subject, and the predicate. The subject is what or who the sentence is about. The predicate is the part of the sentence that expresses something about the subject.**

A sentence must have both a subject and a predicate to be considered a complete sentence. **An incomplete sentence is called a fragment.**

When a writer is really "into" getting his story down on paper, his brain gets going faster than his hand can write. It's common to mistakenly write a fragment instead of a complete sentence. Check your writing for incomplete sentences. They're easy to spot if you know what to look for. Ask yourself: Does this sentence have a subject? Does the rest of the sentence show an action or tell us something about the subject?

For instance, read the following examples:

Coronado galloped out of sight, high into the mountains.

Who is the sentence about?  Coronado
What did Coronado do?      galloped out of sight

Doreen is my best friend.

Who is the sentence about?  Doreen
  What does the sentence tell you about the subject?  my best friend

Make sure you have both parts of the sentence: the subject and the predicate. If you don't, add the information you need.

# Avoiding Sentence Fragments

Name_____Date_____

In the revising process, look for sentence fragments in your writing. Sometimes sentence fragments are the result of rushing to get thoughts down on paper. Other times an author has put end punctuation in the wrong place. Read the following piece. Look for incomplete sentences that don't express complete thoughts. Circle the sentence fragments.

When my grandmother, Rebecca Nix, was a little girl, life was very different than it is now. Since she was born in 1899. There were few modern conveniences. My grandmother lived out in the country, and life was hard.

On laundry day. Rebecca had to help her mother scrub all. The family's clothes by hand. This was an all-day chore, but it had to be done week after week so the family. Would have clean clothes. She hung everything outside on the clothesline. If it rained. She had to gather the clothes and bring them inside and hang them again when the sun came back out. Laundry day was quite tiring, as you can imagine.

Rebecca helped her mother churn butter, sugar peaches, and gather eggs. She checked the hen houses so the fox. Wouldn't sneak in and kill the hens. She got to know the hens as she scattered their chicken-feed each day. Sometimes she had to help her mother kill the chickens and prepare them for the family's dinner. She hated that.

Rebecca's favorite job was milking the cow, Alice. She did this early in the morning, long before the sun came up. Rebecca took a lantern with her to light. The way to the barn. The family cat always accompanied her, hoping to get a squirt or two of fresh milk. Rebecca sat on a small stool and pressed her face against Alice's warm side as she milked. It took her almost 30 minutes to fill the pail for breakfast.

Rebecca worked and played along the banks of the Ocklawaha River with her mother, father, brothers and sister. It is fascinating for me to read her diaries and imagine how different life was in the old days, before most modern conveniences were invented. In some ways, I wish it was possible to visit those old days, myself.

# Who Wants to be a Gazillionaire

## A Five-Minute Play by Melissa Forney

**Regis:** Good evening, ladies and gentlemen. Welcome to *Who Wants to be a Gazillionaire!* Our first contestant tonight is Monica Stillman, from Rochester, New York. Monica was a contestant last night and won over a jillion dollars. (audience cheers) She's here tonight to go for the gazillion. Welcome, Monica.

**Monica:** Thank you, Regis.

**Regis:** Let's get started. For one jillion, two-hundred fifty thousand dollars, what two parts make up a complete sentence? A) Subject and noun   B) Participle and adverb   C) Pronoun and modifier or   D) Subject and predicate?

**Monica:** D, subject and predicate.

**Regis:** Final answer?

**Monica:** Yes, that's my final answer, Regis.

**Regis:** And she's got it. The answer is D, subject and predicate! (audience cheers) Now, for one jillion five-hundred thousand dollars, Which of these is an incomplete sentence:  A) She drove away in a Jaguar   B) Will you come to my birthday party  C) My tired, overworked mother or   D) I'd love a big, juicy hamburger right now  ?

**Monica:** (pause) Let's see...hmmm....A, B and D all have subjects and predicates. C sounds incomplete because there's no verb, no action. I'll say C, Regis. And that's my final answer.

**Regis:** Yes indeed, C it is! (audience cheers) Ladies and gentlemen, Monica Stillman has just won again! (pause) How do you feel?

**Monica:** Nervous! (giggles)

**Regis:** You're doing a great job. Now, for the full gazillion dollars. Remember, you still have two lifelines remaining. Here's the question: What is a sentence called that lacks either a subject or a predicate? Is it  A) a fragment   B) half a sentence  C) a mini-sentence or   D) a little bunch of words?

**Monica:** Oooo, this is tough. I...uh...I should know this....hmmm....Let me see...

**Regis:** You can quit now. You don't have to go for it. You're up to one jillion five-hundred thousand dollars. If you go for it and miss, you'll drop back to a single nickel. That's just *five pennies*, Monica. Big risk. Do you want to stop now?

**Audience:** (cheering) You can do it! Go for it! Go for the money!

## Gazillionaire...continued

| | |
|---|---|
| Monica: | No, I'm going to go for it. (audience cheers) I'd like to phone a friend. I'll call...Norma McCraw. |
| Regis: | Operator, please get Norma McCraw on the line. (pause) Norma McCraw? |
| Norma: | Yes, this is Norma McCraw. |
| Regis: | Regis Filibuster here from *Who Wants to be a Gazillionaire.* Your friend Monica Stillman is stuck on tonight's final question and needs your assistance. Can you help her out? |
| Norma: | Hi, Regis. I'll give it my best shot. I hope I can help her. |
| Regis: | Monica, you have 30 seconds to confer with Norma. Your time begins now. |
| Monica: | Norma, What is a sentence called that lacks either a subject or a predicate? A fragment, half a sentence, a verb, or a little bunch of words? 20 seconds. |
| Norma: | Hi, Monica! Let me see....A sentence that lacks either a subject or a predicate...A fragment. (pause) Yes, that's it. A sentence fragment. |
| Monica: | How sure are you, Norma? 10 seconds. |
| Norma: | 100% sure. Trust me on this one. I learned about complete sentences in writing workshop. Mrs. Taylor always said that sentence fragments are not good because---(buzzer beeps) |
| Regis: | I'm sorry, time is up. Monica, I'll have to ask you for your decision. |
| Monica: | Okay, Regis. I'm going to go with...(pause)...A, a fragment. |
| Regis: | (pause) She's going to go with her friend. Is that your Final Answer? |
| Monica: | Final Answer. |
| Regis: | You're sure? Don't want to change your answer? |
| Monica: | I'm sure. An incomplete or single part of a sentence is called a fragment. |
| Regis: | (dramatic pause) And she's done it!!! She's won a gazillion dollars! |
| Monica: | I've won! I've won! I'm a gazillionaire! |
| Regis: | (to audience) See how easy it is? You, too, could be a contestant on *Who Wants to be a Gazillionaire!* But better brush up on those writing skills. Learning about complete sentences could change your life forever. |

# Sentence Combining

Name_____Date_____

When we talk, we usually speak in long, smooth phrases. When we write, however, sometimes our sentences become short and choppy. The solution? Take several short, simple sentences and combine all of the important information into one gargantuan sentence. For example, these five sentences below are short and immature:

My Mexican hat is large.
It's made out of straw.
The hat is brightly colored.
I bought it on my vacation to Mexico.
It is called a sombrero.

Instead, let's combine all of the important information into one longer, mature sentence:

On my vacation to Mexico I bought a large, brightly colored, straw hat called a sombrero.

Be creative. There are more ways than one to combine the same information:

I have a large, brightly colored, straw sombrero hat that I bought on my vacation to Mexico.

Sentence combining is one of the first things college freshmen learn when they take Writing 101. Why wait till then? Learn this skill to help with your writing now!

Read the following short, choppy sentences:

I have a collection of old marbles.
They are from West Virginia.
There are over 250 marbles in my collection.
I have cat eyes, milkies, steelies, and bolders.
I bought my collection at a flea market.

Now combine the important information into one giant, easy-to-read sentence:

# Practicing Sentence Combining

Name_____Date_____

Practice combining the following short, choppy sentences into longer, more interesting sentences that flow from beginning to end.

My friend Sid has a skateboard.
He lets me borrow it sometimes.
I practice on his ramps.
I can do lots of hard tricks.

_____

_____

_____

My step-dad took me snorkeling.
We went last summer.
I saw an eel and some sea urchins.
I really had a blast.

_____

_____

_____

Carmen talks on the phone for hours.
She is my older sister.
She won't let me use the phone.
I get mad at her.

_____

_____

_____

# Sentence Variety

Name_____Date_____

Sentences that are too much alike sound dull after a while. Experiment with different ways to construct sentences that will give your writing interest and rhythm. Read your piece out loud. Listen for places that are choppy or monotonous. Some of these might be new for you, but here are a few examples of different kinds of sentence construction:

**Subject First:**  <u>Paul Revere</u> rode through the night to warn his countrymen.

**Adjectives First:**  <u>Brave</u>, <u>thoughtful</u>, and <u>patriotic</u>, Paul Revere saved many lives.

**Adverbs First:**  <u>Quickly</u>, <u>quietly</u>, Paul Revere rode through the countryside on his faithful horse.

**Adverbial Phrase:**  <u>Without warning</u>, Paul Revere's horse stumbled and fell.

**Compound Sentence:**  <u>Paul Revere wanted to warn his neighbors</u>, and <u>he did exactly that</u>.

**Short Sentence:**  <u>Paul Revere was amazing</u>!

**Gerund Phrase:**  <u>Riding to warn his neighbors</u> is what Paul Revere is remembered for today.

**Transitional Phrase:**  <u>As Paul Revere shouted his warning</u>, people opened their windows and cheered him on.

**Participial Phrase:**  <u>Slowing his horse</u>, Paul Revere shouted, "The British are coming!" to all who would listen

**Prepositional Phrase:**  <u>Behind the Old North Church</u>, Paul Revere tied up his horse out of sight.

**Subordinate Clause:**  <u>If you want to read a really good story</u>, read about Paul Revere in your history book.

# Amplified Writing

Name_____Date_____

The *New American Heritage Dictionary* defines the word *amplify* as:

amplify (ăm′ plə-fī )1. To make larger or more powerful; extend, increase. 2. To add to, make complete.

**In writing, amplifying means telling more about something. It also means adding more to what has originally been said with a follow-up sentence.**

This simple paragraph below is correct. There's a topic sentence, detail sentences, and a conclusion. All sentences focus on the topic. So, what's the problem? All the sentences focus on the topic, but each one is a totally separate idea from the previous sentence. It needs some **amplification**.

We have such a good time at our annual family reunion. My grandfather takes pictures of everyone to put in a big scrapbook. All the cousins play touch football while the grown-ups watch. There's usually a croquet game going on, too, and my mom sometimes wins. The big highlight of the day is the picnic under the trees. In the afternoon we swing, take walks, talk, or play with the little kids. I hate it when it's time to go home. I wish we had a family reunion once a month, but I have to wait a whole year, till the next Fourth of July.

When you're writing, select a few things your readers might want to know more about. Amplify those thoughts by writing some additional sentences that give details or describe the action. For instance, here's one detail sentence from the example above, followed by several sentences of amplification:

interesting detail: needs amplification!
My grandfather takes pictures of everyone to put in a big
amplification
scrapbook. Each year we look forward to seeing the scrapbook.
amplification                                          amplification
Everyone changes so much. You should see my cool hair from two years ago. Awesome!

# Mission: Possible
A Seven-Minute play by Melissa Forney

**Scene One:  On the north bank of the Seine River, Paris.**

(Music from the movie, *Mission Impossible*. All characters wear dark sunglasses.)

Tape:      Good morning, Ian. Good morning, Team. Your mission, should you choose to accept it, is as follows: Take the enclosed passage, written by a normal kid, and find places in the manuscript where you can amplify the writing. To amplify, as you well know, means to enlarge on, expand, intensify, elaborate, develop, or strengthen. As with any mission, should you or any member of the Mission Possible Force get caught, the agency will deny all knowledge of your existence. (pause) This tape will self-destruct in 5 seconds. (sound effects)

Ian:       What do you think?

Emile:     (French accent) Tough one, eh?

Samantha:  Tough, yes, but I think we can pull it off. Remember Tasmania? We've done this kind of work before.

Ian:       Agreed then?

Everyone:  Agreed.

Ian:       We're in. Dirk, read the highlighted passage.

Dirk:      "Our goal was to set up camp before nightfall. First, we put up our tent. Next, we gathered firewood. After that, we started a fire and cooked our supper. I sat on a split log and gazed up at the stars. It felt good to be in the great outdoors." (silence)

Samantha:  H-m-m...Worse than I thought...Oh, Ian, so many choppy sentences.

Emile:     I told you. Tough one. Every sentence is independent from the others.

Ian:       That's why they called us. If it was easy, they'd have called the FBI.

Dirk:      What's the plan?

Ian:       Divide and conquer. Samantha, you take the tent set up. Emile, firewood and fire. Dirk, you cover supper. Everyone synchronize your watches....(pause)... NOW. We'll meet at the safe house at 0200 hours. All of the information on amplifying is on this disk. Dirk, bring it with you to the safe house. Go silent. I repeat, GO SILENT. (*Mission Impossible* Music)

Mission: Possible....continued

## Scene Two: Safe House, Paris

Ian:          Samantha, Emile. Where's Dirk?

Emile:        He hasn't shown yet.

Ian:          We can't wait.  We'll have to start without him.

Samantha:     Do you think he's had some trouble?

Emile:        He knows the rules. We synchronized our watches. He's late.

Ian:          Samantha, what do you have for us?

Samantha:     Well, Ian, as you know, we started out with *First we put up our tent*. I amplified that thought with these sentences: *It was quite a chore, considering how tired we were after the long hike. Lynn helped me stretch it out, nail down the tent pegs, and fit the supports in the center. It looked like a home away from home.* How's that?

Ian:          You worked in a simile, too? Good going, Samantha. You're a great agent. No sign of Dirk yet. (pause) Emile?

Emile:        You asked for firewood and fire, that's what I amplified: *Next, we gathered dry leaves and branches and lay them in a pile. Before you knew it, we had a roaring fire going, which lit up the campsite and gave off much needed warmth.* Not bad, eh? Magnifique!

Ian:          That's why we hired you, Emile. Only the best. (door slams) Dirk!

Dirk:         (out of breath) I...didn't...know if I could...make it...

Emile:        It's about time! (under his breath)  Imbecile!

Ian:          Did you accomplish your mission? I believe you were to amplify the part about supper.

Dirk:         (upset) Yes...but...the disk you gave me...it's out in the open. It's got all the information on it. I tell you...IT'S GONE!

Samantha:     (alarmed) Out in the open? Where kids can get a hold of the information? Where kids can learn how to amplify their writing?

Mission: Possible....continued

Dirk: It was an accident...I worked on it at the library. When I was done I forgot and left the disk in the computer. When I went back to get it, it was gone! The librarian said she had seen some kid with it.

Emile: Horrors! (under his breath) I knew zees man was an imbecile!

Samantha: Dirk, do you realize what you've done? We won't be needed anymore!

Emile: Who's going to call the Mission Possible Force if kids can amplify their own writing?

Samantha: Dirk, if we can't get that disk back, life in the free world will never be the same. Kids will no longer write sentences that don't relate to each other. They'll learn to amplify their writing like...like...(horrified) *professionals.*

Emile: Kids will learn how to develop, expand, and add details to their sentences.

Dirk: You don't have to tell me. I feel bad enough. They're probably strengthening, intensifying, and elaborating as we speak. Their writing will be as mature as...ours! (desperate) What have I done? What have I DONE?

Samantha: Ian. Why aren't you saying anything? Didn't you hear? The disk is in the open! Kids have the information. There's going to be bedlam. Chaos!

Ian: Don't worry about the disk.

Emile: Don't worry about the disk? Are you crazy? (under breath) He has lost his marbles!

Samantha: Ian, what are you talking about? The disk is *in the open.*

Ian: (Pause) I switched disks.

Dirk: What? Then we're safe?

Ian: I switched the disk. You don't think I could risk letting the real information get out in the open, do you? Let this be an example to you all. (pause) Don't worry about the kids. They don't have a clue. For now, the secret's safe with us. Only the *most mature writers amplify their writing.* Instead of amplifying their own writing they'll need to call on us...the Mission Possible Force.

(*Mission Impossible* music begins)

# Sentence Amplifier

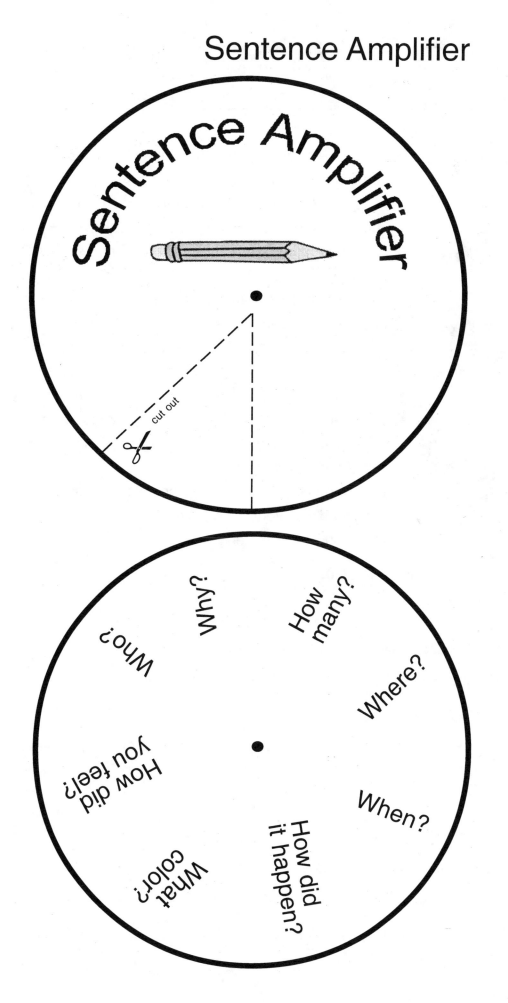

Here's a fun way to remind yourself to amplify your writing. Using a copy machine, copy this Sentence Amplifier onto brightly colored, heavy, craft paper. Cut out both circles. Cut the "Pac Man" wedge out of the first circle. Punch a hole through both centers with a brass brad and fasten the arms of the brad on the opposite side. As you write, spin the Sentence Amplifier to remind yourself of some important questions you can answer or information you can add to your writing.

# Avoiding Tacky Expressions

Name_____Date_____

Let's face it. There are some things that are really tacky when it comes to writing.

For one thing, writing stories about your best friends or other kids in the classroom can be tacky. Some kids make up silly stuff just to impress other kids and don't concentrate on good writing. Make up original characters, instead.

Starting sentences with *And* or *Because* is another thing that can be tacky. It can be done, but it's tricky to do correctly.

Some young writers fill their stories and essays with "filler." These are the kinds of sentences that fill up the page but don't really say anything. Avoid those like the plague.

The list below is a list of "tacky expressions" to stay away from. Instead, use your brain power to think of interesting, well-thought-out sentences.

## Writing No-No's

I have a dog. Do you?

Do you want me to tell you about my dog?

And that's the end of my story.

And I woke up and it was all a dream.

I can't think of anything else to say so....

Don't you think I wrote a good story?

Hi, my name is....

I am going to tell you a story about....

I hope you liked my story.

Bye, gotta go now.

Now, do you have a story to tell me?

The End

Hello. Do you want to read my story?

I'm going to write about....

Okay, here goes....

And now my story is finished.

That's why _____ is my favorite _____. What's yours?

# Before and After Revision

Name_____Date_____

Revision takes our original thoughts and makes them better. Look at this persuasive piece before revision:

## Get Involved

Everyone needs some kind of hobby. Kids sit around, watching television. I think kids need to find something they are interested in. It could be learning to play a musical instrument. It could be learning a new sport. It could be joining some kind of club. These things are good for you. Learning new skills makes you smarter. Kids get bored. They get into trouble. Sports helps develop your body. It keeps you from getting fat. In two or three years you could be really good at whatever you choose to do. Think of something you'd like to study or learn and get involved today.

The writer had some good things to say, but his thoughts were not as clear as they could be. He spent some time revising and organizing his piece. He decided to combine some of his thoughts into longer, more meaningful sentences. He amplified his writing and gave better supporting details. Now his piece is much more convincing and easier to read.

## Get Involved

Everyone needs some kind of hobby to bring pleasure and satisfaction into his life. Too many people just sit around, watching television, complaining that there's nothing to do. I think kids need to find something they are interested in and get involved. If kids spent more time learning something new or participating in sports, they wouldn't be bored or get into trouble.

Playing a musical instrument is an excellent choice, because it expands your mind and creates something beautiful. Being involved in sports helps develop your body and keeps you from getting out of shape. If you join a club, you can help with some great community projects and find a whole new set of friends.

Don't be a couch potato! Think of something you'd like to do and get involved. In two or three years, you could be really good at whatever you choose to do and make a difference in your life.

# NOTES

# Editing

# The Importance of Editing

Name_____Date_____

Class, today we're going to do some editing!

During the creative process, when we're thinking of ideas and trying to get them down on paper, the last thing we want to think about is editing. The most important things to consider at that critical stage are **content** and **creativity**. While our writing is in the revision stage, we don't have to emphasize editing.

**However, if we're going to *publish* a piece that has been through the revision process---adding new information, using better word choice, or answering unanswered questions---all authors should edit their writing pieces carefully.**

**Editing means checking and correcting spelling, grammar, punctuation, left-out words, neatness, and handwriting.**

Writing doesn't have to be absolutely perfect in order to be published and enjoyed, but it shouldn't be unreadable or sloppy, either. When you showcase work that you will publish--retyping, copying over, or putting it in a special binding--it should be reasonably neat and free of obvious errors. We want our readers to be able to read and enjoy our writing without having to trip over gross spelling mistakes or a copy that has so many smudges and crossouts that it cannot be read. Here are some tips to help you edit your writing:

- [ ] Read your paper silently, slowly, and critically. Look for mistakes.
- [ ] Read your paper aloud. Listen for left-out or repeated words.
- [ ] Circle words that are obvious or possible spelling errors.
- [ ] Look up the correct spelling and make corrections in your writing.
- [ ] If you're working on a computer, use the spell-checker.
- [ ] Read your paper backwards to check for spelling errors. It sounds crazy, but your eye catches more errors this way.
- [ ] Look for beginning and ending punctuation.
- [ ] Check for capital letters, commas, and quotation marks.
- [ ] Make sure every sentence has a subject and a predicate.
- [ ] Ask two more writers to read your paper for errors.

# Using Basic Punctuation

Name_____Date_____

Punctuation exists for one reason: to make writing easier to read. It guides the reader through an author's thoughts. Because this is true, authors need to use correct punctuation as a courtesy to the reader. It's a good idea to memorize a few basic rules, and check your writing to make sure you have followed them.

 Put a period at the end of a sentence.

The fading brilliance of the skyrockets mingled with the yellow flicker of summer fireflies.

 Put a question mark at the end of a question.

Will you please quit drumming your fingers on the desk?

 Use an exclamation point to show strong feelings.

Do it now!

 Use commas to separate items in a series.

During the summer I enjoy water skiing, swimming, and camping.

 Start every sentence with a capital letter.

My brother is coming home from college next week.

 Start proper names with a capital letter.

Rebecca asked Gertie and Sarah to go to North Dakota with her.

 Enclose dialogue with quotation marks.

Big Dog Settle took up his fiddle and cried, " Get your dancin' shoes on! Some hot tunes are fixin' to fly out of this fiddle!"

 Start a new paragraph each time someone new starts speaking.

"Would you like to come over for a barbecue?" Uncle Ronnie asked.
"Sure," Rick said. "That sounds like a great idea." He thought for a minute. "What would you like us to bring?"
"Nothing," Uncle Ronnie said. "I've already got everything we need."

# Writing Catchy Titles

Name_____ Date_____

Besides the cover of a book, one of the first connections readers have with a book is its title. Does it capture their attention? Is it about a subject they're interested in? Titles are powerful tools an author uses to make readers want to read what she has written.

How do you write a catchy title? **Ideally, titles should grab the reader's attention without giving away too much information.** As you work on a manuscript you can have a temporary title, called a working title, if you like. Wait until your piece is finished before selecting a final title. **As a rule of thumb, good titles are five words or less.**

Poor Title:   My Friend and I Go Camping
              and Are Chased by a Bear

Better Title:   Terror in the Woods

Learn from the experts. Here is a list of children's book titles. If you listen to their sound and rhythm, you can get a feel for what makes a good title.

| | | |
|---|---|---|
| A Gate in the Wall | Looking For Home | The Bronze Bow |
| A Long Way from Chicago | Madeline | The Cat in the Hat |
| A Wrinkle in Time | Make Way For Ducklings | The Cookcamp |
| A Year Down Yonder | Maniac Magee | The Dog Ate My Homework |
| Bridge to Terabithia | Missing May | The Giver |
| Bud, Not Buddy | No, David | The Hero and the Crown |
| Chicka Chicka Boom Boom | Number the Stars | The Homecoming |
| Curious George | Oonawassee Summer | The Midwife's Apprentice |
| Dear Mr. Henshaw | Our Only May Amelia | The Pigman |
| Dicey's Song | Out of the Dust | The Secret Garden |
| Fourth Grade Rats | Rascal | The Star Fisher |
| Freedom Summer | Roll of Thunder, Hear My Cry | The Stinky Cheese Man |
| George and Martha | Sarah, Plain and Tall | The Upstairs Room |
| Hannah and the Homunculus | Seven Blind Mice | The Vandemark Mummy |
| Hatchet | Shiloh | The View From Saturday |
| Holes | Sing Down the Moon | The Whipping Boy |
| I Have a Dream | Soldier's Heart | Tuck Everlasting |
| I, Juan de Pareja | Sounder | Up a Road Slowly |
| Island of the Blue Dolphin | Summer of the Swans | Walk Two Moons |
| Jacob Have I Loved | The 101 Dalmations | Wayside School is Falling Down |
| Jacob's Rescue | The Bathwater Gang | We Didn't Mean To Go To Sea |
| Little House in the Big Woods | The Blue Tattoo | Where the Wild Things Are |

NOTES

# NOTES

Young Author's
List of Common
Spelling Words

# A

a lot
able
about
above
accident
accuse
across
active
add
address
adjective
admit
adult
adverb
advice
afford
afraid
Africa
African-American
against
age
ago
ahead
aim
air
Alabama
Alaska
all right
alligator
allow
all-star
alone
along
aloud

alphabet
already
also
although
always
amaze
America
American
among
amount
an
anchor
and
angel
angle
animal
ankle
annoy
another
answer
ant
Antarctica
anything
apart
ape
appear
apple
apply
April
area
arena
argue
Arizona
Arkansas
arm
army

around
arrive
art
ash
Asia
ask
asked
Atlantic
athletic
attach
attack
August
aunt
Australia
author
auto
avenue
award
aware
away
awesome
awful

# B

baboon
baby
baby-sit
back
backbone
bad
badge
bag
bagel
baggage
bait
bake

balance
bald
ball
ballet
balloon
ball-point
banana
bank
barn
barnyard
base
baseball
bass
bath
bathtub
batter
bawl
be
beach
beagle
bear
beard
beautiful
beauty
became
because
become
bed
bee
beef
been
began
beggar
begin
behave
behind

being
believe
bell
belly
below
bench
bend
beneath
berry
besides
best
better
between
beyond
bicycle
big
bike
bill
billion
billionaire
bird
bitter
blab
black
blackboard
blame
bleed
blink
blob
blood
blow-dried
blow-dry
blue
blush
board
boat

| | | | | |
|---|---|---|---|---|
| body | bumpy | carbon | cheese | cleanse |
| bogus | bundle | career | cheeseburger | clear |
| bold | burp | careful | cheesecake | clicker |
| bone | bury | carpenter | chew | climate |
| bony | business | carpool | chewing gum | climb |
| book | butter | carrot | child | clip |
| bored | buy | carry | children | clock |
| boring | buzz | cart | chili | close |
| born | by | cartoon | chimp | cloth |
| bother | bye-bye | cash | China | clothes |
| bottom | | cashier | chocolate | club |
| bowl | *C* | cast | choice | cluck |
| box | | casual | choir | clue |
| boxer | cab | cat | choke | clump |
| boy | cabin | catalogue | chomp | clutter |
| brace | cake | catch | chop | coarse |
| branch | calf | cave | choreography | coat |
| brass | California | celebrate | chorus | cobweb |
| bread | call | cell | chosen | cockroach |
| breakfast | called | cemetery | chuckle | cocoa |
| brief | caller | center | cinema | coconut |
| bright | calling | Central America | circle | cocoon |
| brighten | calm | certain | cities | coffee |
| brilliant | camel | chalk | citizen | Coke |
| bring | camera | chalkboard | citrus | cold |
| broccoli | can | champ | city | collar |
| broken | can't | change | civilization | college |
| brother | Canada | chapter | claim | cologne |
| brush | Canadian | charge | clam | Colorado |
| brutal | canal | chart | clang | comb |
| bubble | candle | chatter | clap | come |
| buckle | cannot | chauffeur | class | comedian |
| build | canoe | cheap | classic | comedy |
| bull | cap | check | classmates | comma |
| bully | caption | cheek | classy | command |
| bumblebee | captive | cheerful | clean | commercial |
| | car | | | |

common
communicate
company
complain
complete
compliment
cone
confess
Congress
Connecticut
conquer
constitution
consult
control
cool
corrupt
could
count
country
course
cow
cowboy
cowgirl
crab
crater
crib
crinkle
crisscross
cross
crowd
crude
curly
cursive
cushion
cut

# D

dad
daddy
daily
dairy
damp
dance
dandy
danger
dangerous
dare
daredevil
daring
dark
darken
darkness
dash
date
daughter
dawn
day
daydream
daylight
daze
dazzle
dead
deaf
dear
death
deathly
December
decide
deck
decode
decorate

decrease
deep
deer
defrost
degrade
degree
déjá vu
Delaware
delete
delicate
deliver
demonstrate
deny
depart
deprive
deputy
derby
desk
desktop
despise
details
devote
dew
dial
diary
dictator
did
die
diet
different
difficult
digest
dim
dinky
dinner
dinosaur

diploma
direct
directions
dirty
disappear
disappoint
disaster
disconnect
discount
discovery
discuss
dishonest
dismiss
disobedient
disobey
display
disrespect
distance
distant
ditch
dive
dived
divorce
do
doctor
doe
does
dog
doghouse
dollar
dollhouse
dolphin
donate
donkey
doom
door

dot
double
doughnut
downhill
dragon
dragonfly
drain
drama
drastic
drawback
dress
dribble
drift
drop
dry
dryer
duck
dull
dune
dunk
duration
during
duty
dynamic

# E

each
eager
eagle
ear
earn
earth
ease
east
easy
eat

| | | | | |
|---|---|---|---|---|
| ebony | eve | February | fly | fussy |
| echo | even | federal | folk | future |
| edge | evening | fee | follow | futuristic |
| eel | event | feed | follower | fuzzy |
| eerie | ever | feel | food | **G** |
| effort | every | feet | fool | |
| egg | everyone | fellow | foolish | gadget |
| ego | everything | festival | foot | gallon |
| Egypt | except | fever | forbid | gallop |
| eight | exchange | few | forever | game |
| either | excite | fiction | forget | gang |
| eject | exercise | fiddle | forgive | gap |
| elbow | exhale | field | form | garbage |
| elevator | expose | fiery | fort | garden |
| elect | extreme | file | fortress | gardener |
| electric | eye witness | filler | forty | gargle |
| eleven | eyeball | film | fossil | gas |
| elite | eyelash | final | foul | gasp |
| else | **F** | finalist | four | gaze |
| embarrass | | finally | fox | Georgia |
| emerald | face | finger | fractions | general |
| emotion | fact | fire | frame | generic |
| empty | fail | first | frantic | generous |
| end | fair | firstborn | free | gentle |
| endless | fairly | fish | freeze | genuine |
| endure | fall | fix | Friday | gerbil |
| enforce | false | fixable | friend | germ |
| English | family | flag | fright | gesture |
| enjoy | famous | flatter | from | get |
| enormous | far | flea | fuel | giant |
| enroll | farm | flee | full | gigantic |
| entertain | farmer | flip | fully | giggle |
| envelope | fashion | flirt | function | girl |
| equator | fast | floor | fund | give |
| eraser | father | Florida | fur | given |
| Europe | feather | florist | furniture | glad |

| | | | | |
|---|---|---|---|---|
| gladiator | grime | handle | herbal | ice |
| glass | grip | handstand | here | icicle |
| gleam | gripe | handy | hers | icy |
| glob | grizzly | handyman | herself | Idaho |
| globe | groovy | hang | hesitate | idea |
| glow | gross | hangar | high | ideal |
| glue | group | happen | highway | idiot |
| gnaw | grow | happened | hilarious | if |
| go | growl | harbor | him | igloo |
| goat | grown | hard | himself | ill |
| God | growth | harmony | hip | illegal |
| going | grubby | harp | Hispanic | Illinois |
| gold | grudge | harvest | history | illness |
| gone | gruff | hassle | hobby | image |
| good | guard | hate | hog | imagine |
| good-by | guidance | hatred | hold | imagination |
| gooey | guide | haul | Hollywood | imitate |
| goon | gulp | have | home | immature |
| goose | gum | Hawaii | honey | impact |
| gorilla | gumball | hawk | honor | important |
| got | gurgle | hay | hook | impress |
| grade | guts | haze | hothead | in |
| graduate | gutter | he | hour | inch |
| grammar | | head | how | include |
| grand | **H** | hear | however | income |
| grandfather | habit | heart | howl | index |
| grandma | hack | heartbroken | hug | Indian |
| grandmother | hag | heavy | huge | Indiana |
| grandpa | hail | hectic | hum | indoor |
| grasp | hair | held | human | industry |
| grave | haircut | help | humiliate | infant |
| gravity | half | helper | husband | infect |
| green | hall | helpful | | inflate |
| gremlin | halt | helping | **I** | inhale |
| grew | hand | helpless | I | injury |
| grief | handicapped | her | I'll | ink |

| | | | | |
|---|---|---|---|---|
| inn | jelly | kindergarten | last | lie |
| insect | jerk | kindness | late | life |
| inside | jet | king | later | light |
| instant | jewel | kingdom | laugh | like |
| instead | jiffy | kiss | laughter | lime |
| instruct | jingle | kit | lava | line |
| instructor | job | kitchen | lawn | lion |
| insult | jogger | kite | lay | lip |
| intense | join | kitten | lazy | list |
| international | joke | kitty | lead | listen |
| into | joy | knee | leader | little |
| involve | joyful | knife | leaf | live |
| Iowa | judge | knit | leak | lives |
| iron | juice | knives | lean | living |
| is | juicy | knob | leap | load |
| island | July | knock | learn | loan |
| isn't | jump | knockout | learner | log |
| issue | June | know | leash | long |
| it | jungle | knowledge | least | longer |
| it's | junk | kung fu | leather | look |
| itchy | jury | | leave | loop |
| its | just | **L** | leaves | loose |
| itself | justice | | ledge | lose |
| ivy | jut | label | left | loss |
| **J** | **K** | labor | leg | lost |
| | | lace | lemon | lot |
| jacket | Kansas | lady | length | loud |
| jail | keen | lake | lens | Louisiana |
| jam | keep | lamb | less | love |
| janitor | keg | lame | let | loved |
| January | kennel | lamp | let's | low |
| jar | Kentucky | land | letter | lower |
| jealous | key | lane | level | lowest |
| jeans | kid | language | liberty | lucky |
| jeep | kill | lap | lick | lunch |
| Jello | kind | large | lid | lung |
| | | laser | | |

# M

mad
made
magic
magnet
mail
main
Maine
make
mall
man
many
map
March
Maryland
marine
mark
mask
Massachusetts
mat
matter
may
May
me
mean
meat
meet
melt
memory
men
menu
meow
mess
Mexico
Mexican

Michigan
might
mile
milk
mind
mine
Minnesota
mint
minus
miss
Mississippi
Missouri
mist
misty
mix
mom
Monday
money
monster
Montana
mood
moon
more
morning
most
motel
mother
mouse
move
movie
mow
much
mud
mule
mummy
munch

muscle
must
my

# N

nail
name
nap
napkin
nasty
navy
near
Nebraska
neck
need
nephew
nervous
nest
net
Nevada
never
new
New Hampshire
New Jersey
New Mexico
New York
next
nice
niece
night
nine
no
noise
none
noon
north

North America
North Carolina
North Dakota
nose
not
note
nothing
notice
noun
November
number
nurse
nut

# O

oak
oar
oat
obey
occur
ocean
October
odd
of
off
office
often
oh
Ohio
okay
Oklahoma
old
on
once
one
only

open
opera
orange
orbit
orchestra
order
Oregon
orphan
other
ouch!
our
out
outer space
outside
oven
over
owl
own
ox
oyster

# P

Pacific
package
page
pail
pain
pair
pajamas
pale
palm
pan
pancake
pants
paper
pardon

| | | | | |
|---|---|---|---|---|
| park | piece | print | rail | rid |
| part | pig | prison | rain | ride |
| party | pillow | private | raisin | right |
| past | pin | probably | rake | ring |
| paste | pizza | problem | ram | rip |
| pastry | place | prove | ran | ripe |
| pat | plain | pudding | rap | risky |
| patch | plane | pup | rat | river |
| path | plant | puppy | raw | road |
| pattern | plaster | pure | react | rob |
| pause | plastic | purr | read | rock |
| paws | play | push | reading | rod 'n reel |
| pea | plug | put | real | rode |
| peace | pocket | putt | really | role |
| peach | poem | | record | roll |
| pear | poet | **Q** | red | roof |
| peek | poetry | quack | reed | room |
| pen | point | quake | reel | roost |
| pencil | polar | quart | refugee | root |
| Pennsylvania | pole | quarter | refund | rose |
| penny | pony | queen | relax | rot |
| people | poor | quest | remain | rotten |
| pepper | pop | question | remember | round |
| perfect | popcorn | quick | remove | row |
| perfume | porch | quickly | rent | row boat |
| perhaps | possible | quiet | repair | rude |
| period | post | quit | request | rug |
| permit | pot | quite | rescue | run |
| person | pow | quiz | research | rung |
| pet | powder | | respect | runner |
| photo | power | **R** | rest | rust |
| piano | preach | rabbit | restaurant | rut |
| pick | present | race | retreat | |
| pickup truck | president | raft | review | **S** |
| picture | pressure | rags | Rhode Island | sack |
| pie | pretty | raid | rice | sad |

| | | | | |
|---|---|---|---|---|
| safe | shirt | some | street | teacher |
| said | shoes | someone | string | tear |
| sail | shop | something | strong | teen |
| sale | short | son | student | teeth |
| same | should | song | such | telephone |
| sand | show | soon | suddenly | tell |
| sat | shown | sore | sum | temper |
| Saturday | shut | sound | summer | ten |
| save | sick | south | sun | Tennessee |
| saw | side | South America | Sunday | Texas |
| say | sight | South Carolina | super | than |
| scary | sign | South Dakota | sure | thank |
| school | simple | space | surely | Thanksgiving |
| science | since | speak | surf | that |
| sea | sing | special | surface | that's |
| season | six | spin | sweep | the |
| second | size | spot | sweet | their |
| secret | skate | spring | swim | them |
| see | ski | square | system | themselves |
| seed | skin | stack | | then |
| seen | skip | stairs | **T** | there |
| self | skunk | stamp | table | these |
| sell | sky | stand | tail | they |
| sentence | slap | star | take | thick |
| September | sleep | start | taken | thing |
| set | slip | state | tale | third |
| seven | slow | stay | talk | thirty |
| sew | small | step | tall | this |
| shake | smell | stick | tan | though |
| shall | snack | still | tank | thought |
| shape | snake | stink | tap | three |
| she | snow | stock | tape | threw |
| sheep | so | stood | taste | through |
| shelf | soap | stop | tax | throw |
| shine | sock | store | tea | thumb |
| ship | soft | story | teach | Thursday |

tiger

time

tiny

tip

to

today

toe

together

too

took

tool

tooth

top

touch

toward

town

toy

trade

trap

travel

treat

tree

truck

true

truth

try

tube

Tuesday

tug

turn

turned

turtle

twenty

twice

two

type

# U

ugly

under

understand

until

United States

up

us

use

useful

useless

usually

Utah

utter

# V

valentine

van

vase

vast

vat

vegetable

vent

verb

Vermont

very

vet

video

view

violin

Virginia

visitor

vocal

voice

vowel

# W

wait

wake

walk

walked

want

war

warm

was

wash

Washington

Washington, D.C.

watch

water

wave

wax

way

we

weak

wear

weather

web

Wednesday

weed

week

weight

well

went

were

West Virginia

wet

whale

wheel

when

where

whether

which

while

whip

whisper

white

who

whole

why

wide

wife

wiggle

wild

will

wind

wink

winter

wire

Wisconsin

wise

witch

with

within

without

wolf

woman

wonder

wood

word

work

world

worm

worn

would

write

wrong

Wyoming

# X

Xerox

x-ray

xylophone

# Y

yard

yawn

year

yield

yell

yellow

yes

yesterday

you

you're

young

your

yourself

yo-yo

yummy

# Z

zap

zebra

zero

zigzag

zillion

zing

zip

zipper

zone

zoo

zoom

# Young Author's Additional Words

# Writing Assessment

# Using a Young Author's Assessment Checklist

Name_____Date_____

In life, kids earn many things:

☆ badges in Scouting  ☆ belts in martial arts
☆ scores in ball-playing  ☆ trophies in competitions
☆ ribbons in county fairs  ☆ diplomas in school

In each of these cases, kids have been assessed for their accomplishments. Writing can be assessed, too. Some schools give it a score on a rubric. Others give it a grade. **Writing is assessed to record accomplishment and improvement.**

When you finish a writing piece, you can assess your progress and improvement by using a writer's checklist. The checklist is only a reminder, a place to record specific target skills you've included in your piece. It is by no means a list of items that must be included in every piece. That would be defeating the purpose of your own creativity, style, and imagination. It can be used with fictional narratives, personal narratives, or expository.

Use the writer's checklist to become aware of specific target skills you use naturally or automatically. Use it to spot strengths and weaknesses. If you find there are very few skills to check off, you might want to use the list to help you revise. Remember: your goal as an author is to write so that you impress and involve your reader. Razzle-dazzle them!

For example, let's say you've written the following beginning for a personal narrative:

"Let's go crabbing!" Those are my favorite words to hear on a sunny afternoon with nothing to do but have fun. My cousin Darlene and I gather our crabbing gear: dip-nets, buckets, and frozen chicken necks, and head for the old bridge in New Smyrna Beach, Florida. We think this is the best place to go crabbing because it's shady and not too crowded.

Once there, we tie a chicken neck to each of the crab nets and throw them out on a line attached to the dock. The nets sink into the deep, murky water of the bay and settle down into the silty sand below. This is the domain of the world's tastiest seafood, the Atlantic blue crab.

While we wait for the crabs to take the bait, Darlene and I drink Yoo Hoo drinks and watch the dusty, feathery pelicans that fly overhead before perching on the dock posts. They look like bald old men, begging for handouts of food. The pelicans watch us with hopeful eyes, waiting for the nets to come up.

Now you want to assess your writing for important target skills. Using the young author's checklist, you can check off: grabber opening, personal opinion, dialogue, descriptive writing, sensory words, details, amplified writing, and a simile.

# Young Author's Assessment Checklist

Use this writer's checklist to check and assess your final manuscript.

Author's Name_____Date_____

Title of Piece_____

_____ Address the Prompt
_____ Catchy Title
_____ Grabber
_____ Introduction
_____ Descriptive Language
_____ Personal Opinion
_____ Specific Emotion Word
_____ Juicy Color Word
_____ Dialogue
_____ Simile
_____ Metaphor
_____ Onomatopoeia
_____ Transition Word
_____ Transitional Phrase
_____ Sentences Start Differently
_____ Dialogue
_____ Sizzling Vocabulary Word
_____ "Show, Don't Tell"
_____ Sensory Word
_____ Amplified Writing
_____ Strong Verb
_____ Supporting Details and Reasons
_____ Persuasive Statements
_____ Restating
_____ Conclusion
_____ Takeaway Ending

Comments or Author's Note:

# Assessment Example

Name_____Date_____

This fictional narrative is from a prompt about getting a magic carpet in the mail from your Indian pen-pal. Can you find the target skills that were assessed with the checklist on the following page?

## The Ride of a Lifetime

Never underestimate the power of a plain, brown package. When I rolled out the dusty-looking carpet, it began to vibrate and hum and then started levitating up in the air. I was so shocked, my mouth hung open. I said, "Wha...wha...WHAT IN THE WORLD?" It was at that moment I realized that my Indian pen-pal's gift was NOT just a rug. It was a magic carpet!

The carpet was made of brown, woven fibers, and in the middle there was a picture of a camel. On all four of the outer corners were exotic looking tassels that were colored magenta, cobalt blue, purple, and amber. As I examined the carpet, I noticed a small paper tag tied to the underside. It said, "Dear Pen-Pal. To make the magic carpet GO, pat the camel in the center three times. Then tell the carpet out loud where you want to go. To make the carpet STOP, pull up on the front two corners. Have a great adventure!"

I still couldn't believe what good luck had come to me. I was just an ordinary person, yet I now owned a magic carpet. Unbelievable! I decided that I would take it out for a trial run. After some thought, I decided to go to the exotic, Brazilian jungle. I patted the camel three times, said "The jungle of Brazil," and then WOOSH! The carpet zapped me out of my house and high up into the air. I had to hang on for dear life! The United States flew by, then the ocean, and finally, a mountain range. The carpet suddenly went into a dive and headed for a strange land below. BUMP! We were there.

Before I even opened my eyes, I knew something was different. The air around me was hot and humid. Clouds of steamy fog surrounded my head. I heard the screech of parrots and monkeys. I was in the tropical rain forest! Amazed, I left the carpet on the ground and started to explore. I had to push my way through thick vines and leafy bushes. High up in the trees, I saw snakes and insects I had never seen before. Beautiful flowers grew along the twisting path.

I heard a noise ahead and went to investigate what it was. It sounded like a kitten purring except very, very loudly. I pushed back some branches and came face to face with...a jaguar! He was eating some sort of animal he had killed, and his nose and face were bloody. He looked up from the dead animal and stared straight into my eyes. His gaze chilled my heart. I was frozen to the spot, too scared to move! I wanted to run, but my feet wouldn't move. The jaguar's lips drew back over a mouth full of bone-crushing teeth. A deep, ferocious growl came from his throat.

At that moment, my feet came to life. I heard his threatening hiss behind me and felt his hot breath on my shoulders. I leaped into the air to clear a fallen log. I was going to die!

ZZZZflup!!! My magic carpet flew between the huge cat and me, then under my body, mid-air. As the jaguar pounced, I patted the camel three times and screamed, "HOME!!!!!!!!!!!"

There was a sickening lurch as the carpet shot through the air like a bullet. The scenery whirred by in a blur and the next thing I knew....I was home in my bedroom, still sitting on the carpet, pulling up on the front corners. My arms and legs were trembling. My heart pounded a rapid staccato. I sat panting until my breathing finally returned to normal.

I was alive. The jaguar was gone. I was out of danger! I laughed from relief and joy. After dusting off the carpet, I rolled it into a tight roll and hid it under my bed.

The magic carpet remains hidden there to this day. But who knows? Sometime in the future I might get my nerve up again. With the tap of my fingers, I could be off on another breath-taking, bone-chilling adventure to...who-knows-where?

Assessment Example...continued

Author's Name_____**Heather Fox**_____Date____10/5/01____

Title of Piece____**The Ride of a Lifetime**_____

| | |
|---|---|
| ✓ | Address the Prompt |
| ✓ | Catchy Title |
| ✓ | Grabber |
| ✓ | Introduction |
| ✓✓✓✓✓✓✓ | Descriptive Language |
| | Personal Opinion |
| ✓✓✓✓ | Specific Emotion Word |
| ✓✓✓✓ | Juicy Color Word |
| ✓✓✓ | Dialogue |
| ✓✓ | Simile |
| ✓ | Metaphor |
| ✓✓✓✓ | Onomatopoeia |
| ✓✓ | Transition Word |
| ✓✓✓✓ | Transitional Phrase |
| ✓ | Sentences Start Differently |
| ✓✓✓ | Dialogue |
| ✓✓ | Sizzling Vocabulary Word |
| ✓✓ | "Show, Don't Tell" |
| ✓✓ | Sensory Word |
| ✓ | Amplified Writing |
| ✓✓✓✓ | Strong Verb |
| | Supporting Details and Reasons |
| | Persuasive Statements |
| | Restating |
| ✓ | Conclusion |
| ✓ | Takeaway Ending |

Comments or Author's Note:

I've been trying to improve my descriptive writing. I wanted the reader to imagine what it would be like to be chased by a jaguar.

# NOTES

Resources

# Recommended Reading for Young Authors

Ada, Alma Flor. *The Malachite Palace*. New York: Atheneum, 1998.

Allen, Judy. *Elephant*. Cambridge: Candlewick, 1993.

Armstrong, William H. *Sounder*. New York: Harper & Row, 1969.

Avi. *The True Confessions of Charlotte Doyle*. New York: Orchard, 1990.

Babbitt, Natalie. *Tuck Everlasting*. New York: Farrar, Straus & Giroux, 1975.

Bauer, Marion Dane. *What's Your Story?* New York: Clarion, 1992.

Binch, Caroline. *Gregory Cool*. New York: Dial Books for Young Readers, 1994.

Burnett, Frances Hodgson. *The Secret Garden*. New York: Grosset & Dunlap, 1915.

Burnford, Sheila. *The Incredible Journey: A Tale of Three Animals*. New York: Bantam, 1961.

Cannon, Janell. *Stellaluna*. New York: Harcourt Brace, 1993.

Cleary, Beverly. *Dear Mr. Henshaw*. New York: William Morrow, 1983.

Cole, Joanna. *The Magic School Bus at the Waterworks*. New York: Scholastic, 1986.

Coucher, Helen. *Antarctica*. New York: Farrar, Straus and Giroux, 1990.

Curtis, Christopher Paul. *Bud, Not Buddy*. New York: Delacorte, 2000.

Cushman, Karen. *The Midwife's Apprentice*. New York: Clarion, 1995.

Dahl, Roald. *Charlie and the Chocolate Factory*. New York: Knopf, 1964.

DiCamillo, Kate. *Because of Winn Dixie*. Cambridge: Candlewick, 2000.

Drucker, Malka. *Jacob's Rescue: A Holocaust Story*. New York: Bantam Skylark, 1993.

Edwards, Pamela Duncan. *Barefoot: Escape on the Underground Railroad*. New York: Harper Collins, 1997.

Forney, Melissa. *Oonawassee Summer*. Poulsbo: Barker Creek, 2000.

Fox, Paula. *Slave Dancer*. Scarsdale: Bradbury Press, 1973.

George, Jean Craighead. *Julie of the Wolves*. New York: Harper & Row, 1972.

George, Jean Craighead. *Julie*. New York: Harper Collins, 1994.

Hamilton, Virginia. *M.C. Higgins*. New York: MacMillan, 1974.

Hendershot, Judith. *In Coal Country*. New York: Alfred A. Knoph, 1987.

Hesse, Karen. *Out of the Dust*. New York: Scholastic, 1997.

Hoberman, Mary Ann. *And To Think That We Thought That We'd Never Be Friends*. New York: Crown, 1999.

Hobbs, Will. *Ghost Canoe*. New York: Morrow Junior Books, 1997.

Holm, Jennifer. *Our Only May Amelia*. New York: Harper Collins, 1999.

Howard, Ellen. *Log Cabin Quilt*. New York: Holiday House, 1996.

Joosse, Barbara. *Lewis & Papa: Adventure on the Santa Fe Trail*. San Francisco: Chronicle Books, 1998.

Joseph, Lynn. *The Color of My Words*. New York: Joanna Cotler Books, 2000.

Kim, Lewis. *One Summer Day*. Cambridge: Candlewick, 1996.

Littlesugar, Amy. *Tree of Hope*. New York: Philomel, 1999.

MacLachlan, Patricia. *Sarah, Plain and Tall*. New York: Harper, 1986.

Millman, Isaac. *Moses Goes to a Concert*. New York: Frances Foster Books, 1998.

Morris, Ann. *How Teddy Bears Are Made*. New York: Cartwheel Books. 1994.

Naylor, Phillis Reynolds. *Shiloh*. New York: Maxwell MacMillan, 1991.

Nye, Naomi Shihab. *Sitti's Secrets*. New York: Four Winds Press, 1994.

O'Dell, Scott. *Island of the Blue Dolphins*. New York: Dell, 1960.

Paulson, Gary. *The Island*. New York: Orchard Books, 1988.

Peck, Richard. *A Long Way From Chicago*. New York: Dial, 1998.

Peck, Richard. *A Year Down Yonder*. New York: Dial, 2000.

Ringgold, Faith. *Tar Beach*. New York: Crown, 1991.

Robinson, Barbara. *The Best Christmas Pageant Ever*. New York: Harper, 1972.

Ryan, Pam Munoz. *Amelia and Eleanor Go For a Ride*. New York: Scholastic, 1999.

Sachar, Louis. *Holes*. New York: Frances Foster Books, 1999.

Spinelli, Eileen. *Somebody Loves You, Mr. Hatch*. New York: Bradbury, 1991.

Spinelli, Jerry. *Maniac Magee: A Novel*. Boston: Little, Brown, 1990.

Tanaka, Shelley. *On Board the Titanic*. New York: Heperion Books for Children, 1997.

Vaughan, Marcia. *The Secret to Freedom*. New York: Lee & Low Books, 2001.

Voigt, Cynthia. *Homecoming*. New York: Atheneum, 1981.

Warren, Andrea. *Orphan Train Rider: One Boy's True Story*. New York: Houghton Mifflin, 1996.

Weiss, Nicki. *Where Does the Brown Bear Go?* New York: Greenwillow, 1989.

Williams, Sherley Anne. *Working Cotton*. New York: Harcourt, 1992.

Yolan, Jane. *Moon Ball*. New York: Simon & Schuster, 1999.

# Resources for Teachers

Allington, Richard L. and Patricia Marr Cunningham. *Schools That Work: Where All Children Read and Write*. New York: Harper Collins, 1996.

Atwell, Nancie. *Coming to Know: Writing to Learn in the Intermediate Grades*. Portsmouth: Heinemann, 1990.

Burchers, Sam and Bryan and Sam Burchers, III. *Vocabulary Cartoons*. Punta Gorda: New Monic Books, 1998.

Fletcher, Ralph. *Writer's Notebook: Unlocking the Writer Within You*. New York: Avon Books, 1996.

Fletcher, Ralph. *Live Writing: Breathing Life Into Your Words*. New York: Avon Books, 1999.

Forney, Melissa. *Dynamite Writing Ideas*. Gainesville: Maupin House, 1996.

Forney, Melissa. *The Writing Menu*. Gainesville: Maupin House, 1999.

Fountas, Irene C. and Gay Su Pinnell. *Guiding Readers and Writers (Grades 3-6): Teaching Comprehensive, Genre, and Content Literacy*. Portsmouth: Heinemann, 2001.

Freeman, Marcia. *Building a Writing Community*. Gainesville: Maupin House, 1995.

Gentry, J. Richard and Jean Wallace Gillet. *Teaching Kids to Spell*. Portsmouth: Heinemann, 1993.

Graham, Steve and Karen R. Harris. *Making the Writing Process Work: Strategies for Composition and Self-Regulation*. Cambridge: Brookline Books, 1996.

Graham, Steve and Karen R. Harris. *Teaching Every Child Every Day: Learning in Diverse Schools and Classrooms*. Cambridge: Brookline Books, 1998.

Graves, Donald. *A Fresh Look at Writing*. Portsmouth: Heinemann, 1994.

Hughey, Jane B. and Charlotte Slack. *Teaching Children to Write: Theory into Practice*. Upper Saddle River: Prentice Hall, 2001.

Johnson, Dale D. *Vocabulary in the Elementary and Middle School*. Boston: Allyn and Bacon, 2000.

Kennedy, Marge M. *50 Ways to Bring Out the Smarts in Your Kid*. Princeton: Peterson's, 1996.

Mariconda, Barbara. *The Most Wonderful Writing Lessons Ever: Everything You Need to Know to Teach the Essential Elements*. Scholastic.

Meltzer, Tom. *Illustrated Word Smart: A Visual Vocabulary Builder*.
New York: Princeton Review Publishing, 1999.

Nations, Susan and Mellissa Alonso. *Primary Literacy Centers*. Gainesville: Maupin House, 2001.

Noonday, Peggy Gaye. *Games for Writing: Playful Ways to Help Your Child Learn to Write*.
New York: Farrar, Straus & Giroux, 1995.

Phenix, Jo and Doreen Scott-Dunne. *Spelling Instruction That Makes Sense*. Portsmouth: Heinemann, 1992.

Ray, Katie Wood with Lester Laminacle. *Wondrous Words: Writers and Writing in the
Elementary Classroom*. Urbana: NCTE, 1999.

Ritter, Melissa. *Creating Writers, Spanish/Haciedo Escritores: Espanol*. Portland: NWREL, 2000.

Ritter, Melissa. *Spanish Picture Books*. Portland: NWREL, 2000.

Salpin, Beverly and Doris Seale. *Through Indian Eyes: The Native Experience in
Books for Chldren*. Philadelphia: New Society Publishing, 1992.

Scarffe, Bronwen and Lorraine Wilson. *You Can't Make a Book In a Day: A Practical Guide to
Classroom Publishing*. Victoria: Robert Andersen & Associates, 1988.

Schrecengost, Maity. *Writing Whizardry*. Gainesville: Maupin House, 2001.

Silberman, Arlee. *Growing Up Writing: Teaching Our Children to Write, Think, and Learn*.
Portsmouth: Heinemann, 1991.

Sorenson, Marilou and Barbara Lehman. *Teaching with Children's Books*. Urbana: NCTE, 1996.

Sunflower, Cherlyn. *75 Creative Ways to Publish Students' Writing*. New York: Scholastic, 1993.

Sweeney, Jacqueline. *50 Fantastic Poems With Wonderful Writing Prompts*. Scholastic.

Thomas, Lorenzo. *Sing the Sun Up: Creative Writing Ideas from African-American
Literature*. New York: Teachers and Writers Collaborative, 1998.

Thompkins, Gail E. *Teaching Writing: Balancing Process and Product*. Upper Saddle River: Merrill, 2000.

# Index

# LAGNIAPPE
## A Little Something Extra

Kids need to see good examples of writing written by teachers as well as other students. They need to know your expectations for them--your standards--what you are looking for. I urge teachers to write *for* and *with* their students. When a teacher writes an original piece or writes to a prompt and shares her piece with her students, it is beneficial on several levels:

✓ The teacher becomes part of the writing community.
✓ Children have an example to emulate.
✓ Children can follow an idea from development to finished product.

I recently assigned a writing prompt to a group of fourth-grade students who were preparing for a state writing assessment test. I asked their teachers to write first, and share their examples with their students. This was something they had not often done.

Two weeks later, I returned to assess the students' writing. The kids were waiting for me in the media center, and, one by one, I projected their pieces on the screen with my computerized visualizer. Since their teachers and I had been working with them for several months, I expected to see pleasant, above-average writing.

However, I was in for a big surprise. The writing I saw knocked my socks off--some of the best writing I've seen from fourth-grade students. They described with luscious detail. Their use of dialogue was extraordinary. Strong verbs and action scenes leaped off the page. Their specific emotion words filled me with exhilaration.

They wriggled with pleasure at my reaction. "How did you do this?" I asked. They grinned. One young man volunteered the secret.

"Mr. Royer. He wrote first. He showed us the way."

I carefully examined Mr. Royer's piece, which he had enlarged on a poster-making machine. The answer was as clear before me as a road map. *Mr. Royer's* use of dialogue was extraordinary. *He* described in vivid detail. *His* strong verbs and actions scenes were stunning. *His* specific emotion words reached out and grabbed me. No small wonder his students had made such incredible strides: *they were following his example.*

Yes, some of his students had copied his piece almost word for word. But as they continued to practice, with his encouragement and validation, even those students began to branch out, developing their own ideas and original plots.

Modeling for our students is a good thing. Copying a teacher's ideas is a natural part of the learning process. No one would be concerned if beginning quilting students used the same pattern as their instructor. Voice students learn correct technique by listening to their teacher's voice. Teachers who write for their students pave the way for success.

# Contact Melissa Forney

for

⭐ **Writing Workshops**

⭐ **Teacher Inservice Training**

⭐ **Young Authors Conferences**

⭐ **Motivational Speaking**

⭐ **Keynote Speaking**

**1-800-500-8176**

**crtvendv@aol.com**

Visit Our Web Site

**www.melissaforney.com**

## Workshop Titles

Reading and Writing: Making the Connection
Razzle Dazzle Writing Workshop
Make 'N Take Creative Teaching
Teaching Writing to K-1 Without Losing Your Mind!
Teaching Writing to 2nd-5th Graders: A Recipe for Success
Writing, Brain Dominance, & Learning Styles
Success with Middle Schoolers: And They Said it Couldn't be Done
Pieces of the Quilt: Gathering Family Oral History

## Teachers are saying ....

"I'm writing to you today to tell you that my writing class average was better than I could ever imagine! On a 6 point state writing assessment test, three of my students made a 6.0, five students made a 5.0, five made a 4.5, five made a 4, three made a 3.5, and six students made a 3. Of the six students who made a 3, three were ESE. After attending your workshop and buying two of your books, I went back to my class and worked on reorganizing my writing techniques. I now have writing ideas that work and books that help!"  Barbara, Teacher

"I was lucky enough to attend one of your wonderful workshops. I left the session so excited about teaching--even the teaching of writing--the subject I feared the most."   Kim, Teacher

"I've attended several of your workshops and enjoy using your materials and writing tips with my Gifted students. Our writing assessment scores continue to climb!"   Drema, Teacher

"Melissa Forney's workshop was one of the best I've ever attended."   Patti, Teacher

"I use your books more than any other teacher resource."   Melissa,  Teacher

# If you liked *Razzle Dazzle Writing*, try these other Maupin House resources.

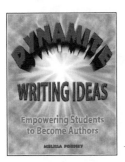

## Dynamite Writing Ideas

**Empowering Students to Become Authors**

**Melissa Forney**

*"The lesson plans in* Dynamite Writing Ideas *are a must for every classroom teacher. They help teachers plan for the entire year." —Louisiana teacher*

*Dynamite Writing Ideas* supports your writing program with ideas, strategies and handy reproducibles that save you time—from August setup through end-of-year publishing.

**ISBN 0-9329895-18-5, 119 pp. Bibliography. Item #MH 29 • $17.95**

## The Writing Menu

**Ensuring Success for Every Student**

**Melissa Forney**

*"The explosion of ideas makes this book exciting as well as teacher-friendly." —Dr. Carolyn Musslewhite*, Special Communications

Apply the latest research on multiple intelligences in your classroom with this standards-based resource. Narrative and expository prompts, activities, reproducibles, story planners, oral literacy games, manipulatives and instructional strategies make this one an all-around winner. Grade-appropriate target-skill lists ensure accountability.

**ISBN 0-929895-33-9, 132 pp. Index, Bibliography. Item #MH 49 • $17.95**

## Building a Writing Community

**A Practical Guide**

**Marcia S. Freeman**

*"Even with all the books on the writing process out there, this book deserves a place in most professional libraries for use in school staff development and in preservice teacher education....The candid flavor will be popular with teachers. Especially helpful is the space devoted to understanding writing in different genres and the different techniques involved... well written and well organized for easy use." —Wendy C. Kasten, Kent State University*

If you want to create a community of writers who love to write and speak the language of writers, you'll love this book. The classroom-tested techniques satisfy young writers' need for structure and content while offering them freedom to develop their style, repertoire and voice. More than 350 models, lessons, procedures, activities and 37 reproducibles help schools and districts teach writing effectively.

**ISBN 0-929895-13-4, 242 pp. Index, Bibliography. Item #MH 24 • $23.95**

*(Continued on the following page.)*

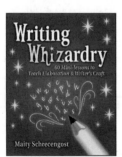
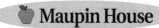